If You Don't Know Where You're Going, You'll Probably End Up Somewhere Else

Search

Finding a Career and Getting a Life

David P. Campbell

Sorin Books Notre Dame, Indiar

What students are saying about
If You Don't Know Where You're Going, You'll Probably End Up Somewhere Else:

I loved the frank and realistic language of *If You Don't Know Where You're Going. . . .* It made me want to reassess my goals and make sure they were attainable. But, at the same time, I also felt the impulse to let go of all future plans and leave my life open for anything.

Dee Lind
Senior, Marian High School, Mishawaka, Indiana

This book is great! David Campbell gives very wise advice that makes me feel more comfortable with and confident about leaving high school and starting the adventure of college.

Georgene Clements
Senior, Saint Gertrude High School, Richmond, Virginia

We tend to rush through everyday without thinking about all the choices we are making. *If You Don't Know Where You're Going . . .* helps show that each decision is important and that our surroundings mean more than we think.

Maggie O'Neill
Senior, Immaculate Conception Cathedral School, Memphis, Tennessee

Dr. Campbell's philosophy is both accessible and practical to young readers. *If You Don't Know Where You're Going . . .* could be helpful to anyone needing an easy-going guide to arranging their priorities.

Rob Funkhouser
Senior, Seton Catholic High School, Richmond, Indiana

If You Don't Know Where You're Going . . . can show you all the open doors on your journey through life, no matter your age.

Emily Coats
Trinity Junior High School, Fort Smith, Arkansas

Instead of focusing on the expectations and standards that others set for you, *If You Don't Know Where You're Going . . .* allows you to stop and look at yourself and what you have to offer to the world. The book showed me how to assess my own self-worth through my own talents and skills instead of just living my life as another number.

Anna Hill
Senior, Saint Gertrude High School, Richmond, Virginia

David Campbell gives great advice on using goals as a tool for creating the pathway for your future. I recommend this book for those who maybe unsure of their future plans. This gives them some motivation to plan and be able to reach their goal.

Toraneka Hampton
Senior, Immaculate Conception Cathedral School, Memphis, Tennessee

This book gives excellent advice to students entering college and the working world.

Luci Osby
Senior, Saint Gertrude High School, Richmond, Virginia

This book is 128 pages of powerful motivation and great advice on how to prepare for the future with a solid plan and realistic goals.

Colin Van Es
Senior, Marian High School, Mishawaka, Indiana

You cannot control everything that occurs in your life, but David Campbell certainly helps to point you in the direction in which you can decide where your future lies. Your future is in your hands, whether you know it or not, and *If You Don't Know Where You're Going . . .* will show you how to decide where to go and how to get there.

John Purcell
Senior, Seton Catholic High School, Richmond, Indiana

This book is great. It helped me to provide more options for myself and try more things in life.

April Stec
Trinity Junior High School, Fort Smith, Arkansas

The book reminds readers that life happens not to them, but because of them. Rather than reveal the magic formula for lifelong fulfillment, Campbell's questions equip readers to find their own answers.

Christine Donovan
Senior, University of Notre Dame

Campbell offers humorous and interesting, yet practical, advice to help guide you through that looming question concerning where you are headed in life.

Erin Hollister
Senior, Bethel College

© 1974, 2007 by Ave Maria Press, Inc.

www.sorinbooks.com

ISBN-10 1-933495-06-5 ISBN-13 978-1-933495-06-4

Cover and text design by Brian C. Conley
Printed and bound in the United States of America.

Library of Congress Cataloging-in-Publication Data
    Campbell, David P.
      If you dont know where youre going, youll probably end up some-
where else : finding a career and getting a life / David P. Campbell.
        p. cm.
     ISBN-13: 978-1-933495-06-4 (pbk.)
     ISBN-10: 1-933495-06-5 (pbk.)
     1. Vocational guidance. 2. Success. 3. Happiness. I. Title.

   HF5381.C254 2007
   650.1--dc22

                        2006037625

You have to take LIFE as it happens, but you should try to make it happen the way YOU want to take it.

—An old German saying

Contents

"Cheshire-Puss," said Alice, "would you tell me, please, which way I ought to go from here?"

"That depends a good deal on where you want to get to," said the Cat.

"I don't much care where—" said Alice. "Then it doesn't matter which way you go," said the Cat.

"—so long as I get somewhere.' Alice added as an explanation. "Oh, you're sure to do that," said the Cat, "if only you walk long enough."

—**Lewis Carroll**
Alice's Adventures in Wonderland

CHAPTER ONE

The Road to Somewhere

• •

Unless you know what you want from life, you are not likely to stumble across it—but how do you know what you want? Especially if you are in some "the future-is-misty" stage and are not quite certain where you are heading. How do you decide what will be important in your future?

From interviews with hundreds of people about their hopes and plans, and from surveys of thousands of people about their careers, I have learned that what most people want out of life, more than anything else, is *the opportunity to make choices.*

What We All Want Is Choices

The worst possible life is a life without choices, a life barren of the hope of new things, a life of blind alleys, often leading to hopelessness. In contrast, the most pleasant life is the life filled with future opportunities.

For example, here are several possible outcomes of life; which of them appeal to you?

- Having an interesting job.
- Having a good marriage.
- Running your own company (or your own laboratory, or your own ranch, or your own newspaper).
- Living overseas in the beautiful village by the sea.
- Spending time with interesting friends.
- Having a comfortable home in the country.
- Living in a modern apartment in the heart of an exciting city.

The greatest tragedy in LIFE is to have no options, to have no choices.

- Having enough free time and money to travel to interesting places.
- Being part of a close-knit, loving family
- Staying in good physical condition.
- Having people come to you because you are an expert.
- Making enough money to educate your children, purchase beautiful art, and contribute funds to others who are in need.
- Working in an important government post, influencing what is happening in your country.
- Producing a great work of art, or making an important scientific discovery, or devising a better master plan for a city, or making a run-down farm profitable.

If you are like most people, many of these might appeal to you. You might even answer, "I would like to have almost all of those things happen to me at one time or another." What you are saying is that you want to have many potential opportunities so that you can pick and choose.

That is what this book is all about—creating opportunities for yourself. Sooner or later, you will realize that *the greatest tragedy in life is to have no options, to have no choices.* Consequently, when you are planning your future, you should plan it in a way that will give you a range of choices. This approach is particularly important if you are not certain right now what you want to do. Some people, when they are uncertain, have a tendency to do nothing, and this substantially restricts their future choices. Even if you do not know what you want to do in the long run, there are actions that you can take in the short run that will give you more choices when the long run gets here.

11

To Create Choices, You Must Have Goals

How can you be certain that you will have future choices? By setting goals so that you do not drift aimlessly. But they have to be the right kind of goals. The average person, when asked what they want from life, replies with fairly specific goals, such as "a good education, a good job, a good marriage, a loving family, a pleasant home, travel, money, success."

For two reasons, such aims are not very useful in helping you plan a satisfying life. First, these goals are fixed, unchanging, while life is just the opposite. To say, for example, that you want a good job implies that there is a job somewhere that will keep you happy indefinitely. Or to yearn for a good marriage implies that once you have found the right person to marry, you will live happily ever after.

Well, it doesn't work that way. *Practically all goals tarnish with time if they are not renewed in some way.* A job that is exhilarating during the first year becomes less so after five years; without renewal, it becomes an automatic, perhaps humdrum activity after ten years, and a prison after twenty. The same for a marriage. The divorce rate, perhaps the best indication of marriage failures, is almost fifty percent, demonstrating that even relationships of love ("till death do us part") can weaken and change with time if there is no renewal.

The second reason that such specific goals are not the best focus for our strivings is that, once attained, they no longer seem so important. To earn a degree, to be promoted, to make $100,000, to marry the most important person in the world, to win a gold medal, to reach a quota—these are the carrots that we strive for, and they are pleasant at first, extraordinarily so, but without continual growth, they pale. The poet Emily Dickinson wrote, "Success is counted sweetest by those who ne'er succeed;" Adam Smith said essentially the same thing in *The Money Game,* a fascinating book on what motivates people to play the stock market: "No specific goal can sustain one for very long after it is achieved."

Goals are useful, to be sure—much of this book is devoted to them—but they should not be viewed as end products. Goals are useful only as they help move from here to somewhere else.

Like Alice, most of us think we want to go "somewhere," and it takes some experience to learn that, in life, there is no "somewhere." *There is only the road to somewhere and we are always on the way.*

Where do we learn to think of life as having "somewheres," as having places that once we reach, we will always be happy? Through the media. *Much of what we know of life, we learn from television, plays, books, and movies.* Much of that is educational, sometimes in peculiarly useful ways. John Kenneth Galbraith, the Harvard professor who was President John F. Kennedy's Ambassador to India, reported in his book, *Ambassador's Diary,* that when he arrived in India, he was expected to review a large contingent of Indian troops. He had no warning and no prior experience in reviewing troops. How did he know what to do? As he put it, "For my protocol, I drew heavily on old television shows. . . ."

Although the media have educated us in many useful ways, they have also misled us into thinking that the world is full of endings, some happy, some sad, but always endings.

13

There is only the road to somewhere and we are always on the way.

The movie ends, the television show ends, the novel ends, the play ends. That is not the way the world is. In life there are no endings. No matter how pleasant of painful the weekend was, the cast always gets up on Monday morning and goes about its business. In a movie, the sun may set, the moon may rise, the honeymooners may walk hand in hand down the lane to a climactic fade-out, but, in real life, they will awaken to an average day that may start with the scratchy realization that here they are in this expensive resort with no toothpaste and they cannot get the taste of last night's spicy dinner out of their mouths.

To give up the concept of "endings" is one of the most important steps in learning to plan realistically. Many people have trouble accepting this, and maybe an example will help.

One painful realization suffered by a young woman who has aimed her life toward happy endings ("a good marriage, a great job, a loving family, and a nice home") comes when the children have left home and she is left alone, when she realizes that she hates her job, the house that needs to be cleaned weekly is only a millstone around her neck, and her husband is totally absorbed in his work and his golf game, an absorption that may leave his wife excluded. For a woman in that position, happy endings are pretty flat.

The same thing happens to men; the scenario may be slightly different, but the outcome is the same. *Life is complicated—that's why it is fun,* but we need a way of thinking about it that captures this complexity and one that allows us to plan our goals accordingly.

Think of life in this way. Instead of happy endings and "somewheres," think of life as a long, never-ending pathway stretching our ahead of you, with many other pathways branching off to either side. The pathway you are on now represents the lifestyle you are now living; the branching

Drink and dance
    and laugh and lie.
Love the reeling midnight through.
    For tomorrow we shall die!
(But, alas, we never do.)

—**Dorothy Parker**
"The Flaw in Paganism"

. . . You'll Probably End Up Somewhere Else

pathways represent new directions you might take—new jobs, new hobbies, and new places to live. One new pathway might be labeled, "be a cartoonist," and if you have the proper talents and energy, you might choose to start down that pathway. Soon you would reach a fork where one branch would be labeled "freelance cartoonist," and the other, "regularly employed." You will have to choose, and your choice will have considerable influence on your further options because the future pathways leading from the two different branches will not always be the same.

Each branching pathway has a gate, and the gate will be open for you only if you have the right credentials. Consequently, when you come to new pathways, two factors will determine whether you will leave the pathway you are on now and start down a path leading in a new direction. The first factor is whether the pathway is open to you, which will be determined by your credentials; the second factor is whether or not you want to go through the gate, even if it is open. The first factor—your credentials—is the more important because if the gate is not open for you, you have no choice, no matter how badly you wish to follow the new pathway. Consequently, your main strategy in planning a life with maximum opportunities is to accumulate the best credentials possible—or, as I call them, assets—so that the maximum number of pathways will be open to you. *You want the choice to be in your hands, not the gatekeepers' hands.*

To Reach Your Goals and to Expand Your Choices, You Must Have Assets, the More the Better

These pathways and gates are only imaginable, of course. They represent the choices you will have in life. They might be labeled with occupations: doctor, lawyer, farmer, chef; or with places to live: big city, small town, the country, overseas; or with general lifestyles: married with a large family, famous with lots of money, a powerful politician, a quiet, comfortable life in a small village.

Whether any of the pathways will be open for you depends on your assets—on such factors as your education, your work experiences, your skills, perhaps your family connections, even your appearance and, above all, your health. If, for example, you want to enter the pathway marked "medical school," you will need to take the right courses in college, you will need to earn good grades, and you will need to have impressed someone who is reasonably important so that they will write a good letter of recommendation for you. If you want to go down the path marked "farming," because of the high cost of entry, you will probably have to inherit a farm (or marry someone who will). If you want to live overseas, you will need to have an occupation that is exportable, such as entertainer, international manager, language translator, or scientist, you will probably need to speak a foreign language fluently, you will need to grow up in a family that has foreign connections, or you will need a substantial amount of imagination, persistence, and luck. The point is, *most pathways are open only to people with the right combination of assets, along with the necessary motivation.*

For most people the pathway ahead is usually misty. You cannot be exactly certain where your current pathway is leading, and you certainly cannot see all possible branching pathways that might appear in the future. However, once you realize that whether or not a specific gate will be open for you depends on the assets you have, then—even if the future is misty—you can begin creating future choices now by increasing your assets, even if you are not certain which future pathways you may wish to follow. You will at least have choices, and the more assets you have, the more future pathways that will be open for you, and therefore the more choices you will have.

What opens the gates to new pathways? The next chapter is devoted totally to that question, and you should study it closely. Generally, what it says is that *education* opens new pathways, *experience* opens new pathways, *talents* open new pathways, *well-connected friends and family* open new pathways, *good health* opens new pathways (or at least keeps some from closing), and *personal characteristics* such as *physical or mental abilities, creativity, persistence, leadership* and *good work habits* open new pathways.

Your age may also have some impact on whether gateways will be open to you. Early in life, we start passing gateways leading off from our route and, unless we see them, have the right assets, and the desire to enter them, some of them will be forever closed to us. For example, the pathway "Be a concert pianist" comes along early in life, even as early as six years of age, and most of us shoot right by it without realizing (or caring) that that pathway (i.e., that occupation) is probably forever closed to us. Thus, some decisions have to be made quite early in life although, remember, no decision is fixed. Even an early decision to

18

devote yourself to the piano is only a decision to start down that pathway. Other pathways will continue to appear, some with open gates, some with locked gates, again depending on your credentials.

There is no use in fretting much about your age you cannot change it and you cannot slow aging down.

At the other extreme, some pathways do not come along until you have lived a while. Sometimes the restrictions are formal—for example, you must be at least thirty-five years old to be President of the United States—but generally the restrictions on age eliminate people without appropriate experience. For example, most influential politicians are in their fifties and sixties, not because of any formal restrictions, but because it requires many years of living to build a political base that can help in winning elections.

There is no use in fretting much about your age; you cannot change it and you cannot slow aging down. What you can do is make certain that when you are old enough to considering entering a new pathway, you will have the necessary credentials for opening that gate—and that takes planning.

19

Planning

I once asked a successful man, while interviewing him about his career, "What led to your success? How did you make it to the top?"

"A lot of luck," he answered, "but a lot of planning too. I have always been a planner."

"Tell me about that . . . when did you start planning?"

"I can tell you exactly when because I remember it as if it were yesterday. I was in college, living in a dormitory room with a boy from Iowa. He came in one night while a bunch of us were sitting around, talking about life. I could tell he was excited, but he did not say anything until everyone else left. Then he blurted out, 'my folks just got rich!! My mother called tonight—she walked out to the mailbox this morning and found a check for a half-million dollars!'"

If you **want**
something to
happen,
make a space
for **it.**

—A savvy college student

"My reaction, after the initial astonishment, was only barely concealed envy. I asked him how it happened.

"He said, 'I don't exactly understand, but I guess my dad bought some stock in a small company years ago, and then just kind of forgot about it. The company has just been bought out by a larger company, and this is our share.'

The man I was interviewing continued, "That night I lay in bed awake a long time, thinking, 'Why was it his family and not mine? Why him and not me?' Finally, I tried to analyze it in a systematic way.

"I thought to myself, 'what could possibly happen in my life to bring me such a windfall?' and bleakly I realized that there was nothing. I had no old stock that would shoot

Do not wait until you are thirsty to dig a well.

臨渴掘井

—Chinese proverb

臨渴掘井

upwards in value nor, as far as I knew, did my family. I had no land where someone might suddenly find oil; I had no paintings that might turn out to be by Old Masters; I had no talents that someone, somehow was going to miraculously discover overnight to make me famous—I had nothing special going for me. And right there in that dormitory bed I said to myself, 'Charlie, if you want something to happen in your life, you have to plant some seeds, and you had better plant a lot of them because you never can tell which ones will sprout.' Since then, I have always been a planter of seeds. A few of them have sprouted, and here I am."

Later on, a university student put it to me more succinctly. This young woman, a likeable, alert, and enthusiastic striver, said to me, "If you want something to happen in your life, Professor, you have to make a space for it." She put her hands straight out in front of her, palms together, and started forcing them slowly apart, as though she had stuck them into a bale of cotton, and was slowly forcing them apart, making a bigger and bigger space in the cotton. "You see, you have to make a space for it . . . for whatever it is you want."

If you want milk,
there is no sense
sitting on a milk stool
in the middle
of a field,
waiting for a COW
to back up to you.

—A Midwestern farmer

Both of these people were planners; they made things happen in their lives, either by planting seeds or pushing aside the cotton. They did not sit idly by, waiting for life to happen to them. They went out looking, they made plans, and then they took actions.

Here are some comments that should help you make better plans.

1. Planning is a matter of probabilities, which means that sometimes your plans will work out, and sometimes they will not—you can save yourself a lot of grief by realizing that sooner rather than later. *Nothing in life is a sure thing, and any plans that you make for the future will have to deal with uncertainly.* Once you realize that, several other conclusions are apparent. First, there are steps you can take to raise your probability for success. Second, you had better have some alternatives in case your first plan is unavailable. Third, any given plan can fail, and you had best prepare for that possibility also.

22

2. Your planning should cover different time spans, such as one hour, one week, one year, or ten years. Obviously, planning has to be much different if you are thinking about next year as opposed to ten years from now. You can, and should, plan ten years ahead but you cannot do it with much precision because there are too many uncertain factors. As Winston Churchill once said when speaking of planning the affairs of the British Empire, "*One must always look ahead, but it is difficult to look farther than you can see.*" You can, and should, plan for one hour ahead also; you can do that with substantial precision, but of course any one single hour will not have much impact on your life. (Although several single hours stacked together, well planned and well executed, can be an excellent contribution to your future opportunities.)

Although there will be much uncertainty in your life over the next ten years, one thing that you can count on with absolute certainty is that ten years from now, you will be ten years older. If you are reading this book at age seventeen, in the next ten years of your life, you will probably complete your formal education, leave home, marry, start your first job, and switch jobs at least once (according to the averages). The odds of all of those things happening are high; what planning are you doing for them now?

If you are reading this book at age thirty-seven, in the next ten years, you may reach the peak of your occupational life, your income may reach a maximum and level off, you may purchase a home, your children will probably be teenagers (and they will likely be planning their college educations and leaving home), and the aging of your body will become more evident, especially if you have poor health habits. You will probably have less energy and endurance

The winds of grace
may be blowing,
but it is up to US
to set
the sails.

—A Norwegian
ship's captain

than you have now. Distressing, perhaps, but a fact and one
that you should plan for.

24 Goal Planning

You can categorize your goals roughly as follows:

- Long-range goals, over the horizon;
- Medium-range goals, the next chapter in your life;
- Short-range goals, the coming year;
- Mini-goals, thirty days ahead; and
- Micro-goals, the next fifteen minutes.

Long-range goals are those concerned with the overall style of life that you wish to live—the type of job that you
want, whether you wish to be married, the kind of family

that you want, where you will be living, basically the general situation that you wish to live in. Although you should develop some overall idea of what you are after, do not try to plan long-range goals in detail because too many changes will come along. Have an overall plan, but keep it flexible.

Medium-range goals are goals covering the next five years or so; they cover the particular kind of training or education you are seeking, or the next step in your career. You will have more control over these, and you can tell along the way whether or not you are achieving them and modify your efforts accordingly.

Short-range goals are goals covering the period from about one month to one year from now. You can set these goals quite realistically and can tell fairly soon whether you are reaching them. Do not set impossible goals for yourself. While you always want to stretch yourself, you do not want to become discouraged. *Aim realistically and optimistically*, but then try hard to achieve your aims. If you fail, try again. If you fail again, try to fail smarter. Persistence is necessary for success in achieving most worthwhile goals.

It was a day like today when MARCO POLO left for China. What are your plans for today?

—Loesje International poster

25

Mini-goals are goals covering from about one day to one month. You will have much more control over these goals than you do over the longer-term goals. You can plan out a program for the next week, or the next month, and your chances of carrying it out—assuming your goals are reasonable and your motivation is strong—are good. If you find that you have planned too ambitiously, you can modify it for the period after that. By thinking in shorter hunks of time, you will have far more control over each hunk.

> Everyone is trying
> to do something big,
> not realizing that LIFE
> is made of
> little things.

> —Frank A. Clark

Micro-goals cover the next fifteen minutes to one hour. Realistically, these are the only goals that you have direct control over. Because of this direct control, micro-goals, even though they are modest in impact, are extraordinarily important in your life, for it is only through these micro-goals that you can attain your longer goals. As the old adage says, "A journey of a thousand miles begins with a single step." If you do not make any progress toward your long-range goals in the next fifteen minutes, when will you? The following fifteen minutes? The fifteen minutes after that? Sooner or later, you are going to have to pick fifteen minutes, take that single step, and get going.

If you plan your micro-goals well, and then make progress toward them—"I'm going to start that report right now," "I'm going to learn that new technique right now," "I'm going to learn ten new words in that foreign language right now," "I'm going to make that sales call right now"— your long-range goals will be more achievable.

In general, the bigger the goal, the more it will impact your life but the less direct control you will have over achieving it. If, for example, your long-range goal is to become a famous pianist, there is little you can do about that today—you cannot go out a brew up a little instant fame. In contrast, you have a lot more control over micro-goals. You can say to yourself, "In the next hour, I am going to master one line of the Beethoven concerto," and you can do it. One mastered line will not make you famous, but it is a step—and a necessary one—in the right direction.

The point is that the only goals you have direct control over are the modest, little goals; the trick of planning a successful life is to stack together these smaller goals in a way that increases your chances of reaching the long-range goals that you really care about.

Although I was a World Champion, I still had PLENTY of learning to do, and the next three years were a process of testing and REFINEMENT.... Life from now on would be a matter of incremental improvements, of SEEKING the tiniest margin that might separate me from the other ELITE riders.

—**Lance Armstrong**
It's Not About the Bike
He went on to win the Tour de France for the sixth time.

3. Plan for intensity; in at least one area of your life, be intense. Focus strongly on something, whether is your job, a hobby, or some group activity such as choral singing. Be good at something, good enough so that you can take quiet pride in knowing that you are a valuable person, that you can do at least one thing well. To do this requires *dedication, determination,* and *persistence.* You cannot be dedicated, determined, and persistent in all areas, but do select one area and excel. If you pick the right area—and the next chapter has a lot to say about that—good things will happen to you. If you do not know what that area for you should be right now, don't worry, experiment, try several until your passion becomes evident. Maybe you should even develop a useful obsession. As one person said to me once, "I believe in obsessions; they give me more ways to find happiness."

If you do not climb the mountain, You will not see the plain.

—Chinese proverb

不上高山
不顯平地

不上高山，
不顯平地

4. Plan some diversity in your life, even while you are focusing on one area. Life is full of changes, and the best protection against catastrophic change is diversity in your talents. Perhaps you are already skilled with computers: now learn to write well, play a musical instrument, work with woodworking tools, tend houseplants to keep them healthy, or sell products to other people. Again, experiment, and keep these experiments with new areas of talents going on all of your life. *Do not become narrow and stagnant.*

5. Plan for gradual improvement, not spectacular leaps. Practically everything worthwhile in life is achieved in small steps. Education is accumulated gradually, babies grow up one day at a time, beautiful gardens are designed and grown slowly, talents are honed, relationships are forged, deep affection is created, all very gradually. Each of our lives is a series of gradual campaigns on many fronts— job, family, talents, friends, our physical environment—to make a better life, and few campaigns move quickly.

Nature provides many guidelines here. A slow and steady stream of water will, in time, erode the hardest rock; a small, insignificant sprout will, in time, slowly and imperceptibly turn into a mighty oak; an almost unnoticed child will, in time, grow up to be an independent adult. *Recognize the gradualness of life and the power of "in time."*

A final comment on planning: to plan, you must have information. You must know something the specific details of your plans. If you are planning your schooling, you must know something about the educational options available to you, no matter what your age. If you are planning your future career, again no matter what your age and where you are now, you must know something about various occupational opportunities. If you are planning your future home, you must know something about real estate, housing, and interior design.

To accumulate knowledge on any subject, you have to do some digging. You have to read books, magazines, pamphlets, anything relevant that you can get your hands on. Surf the Web. Talk to knowledgeable people, a wide range of them. Seek out interviews; you will be surprised at how willing experienced people are to talk about their experiences to someone who appears to be truly interested. Ask an ophthalmologist, "What's it like to be an ophthalmologist?" You will be surprised, perhaps even delighted with what you learn.

It's the same with people who come from different cultures and different countries. Ask them about their lives, and the different activities that go on in their country. What does their land look like? What kind of people live there? How do they make their living? How is their country different from yours? Curiousity is valuable.

You also have to accumulate some life experiences for yourself. Virtually anything that educates you is worthwhile, so seek out experiences in the areas where you are trying to plan. The basic point is you cannot make good plans until you have some raw material to plan with. You need knowledge and experience. Happily, it is almost always interesting, and often fun to accumulate both.

For unto every one that
hath shall be given,
and he shall have abundance:
but from him
that hath not,
even that which he hath
shall be taken away.

—Matthew 25:29 (ASV)

CHAPTER TWO

If You Have It, Use It

●●

Do You Want to Be Happy?

To be able to live the kind of life you want, you need to have as many choices open to you as possible. *To make choices, you must have assets*—you must have something going for you. Assets include good health, a good education, a wide array of talents, broadening experiences, and helpful family and friends. Even if you do not know now exactly what you want out of life, you can concentrate on building your assets. The more you accumulate, the more choices you will eventually have, no matter what direction you choose to go in.

You can evaluate your assets in much the same way that a bank or corporation does, by adding up your strong points—your assets—and subtracting your weak ones. The only difference is that while a commercial organization looks at dollars, that is, financial assets, you should be looking at your psychological assets. In the following pages, various psychological assets are discussed. As you read about them, take stock of your own situation—which of these assets do you have? Which ones are under your control and thus can be increased? Which ones are not under your control and thus must be planned around?

The assets that are going to have the greatest impact on your future choices are your

1. Talents and skills
2. Intellectual Intelligence
3. Emotional Intelligence
4. Education
5. Friends
6. Family
7. Experiences
8. Appearance
9. Health

The more you have going for you in each of these categories, the more future choices you will have.

YOUR TALENTS AND SKILLS

Your talents and skills are important ingredients, perhaps the most important ones, in opening up new pathways for you. *Talents include general abilities* such as musical, mathematical, and mechanical talent. *Skills include specific abilities* such as playing the piano, programming a computer, and working with tools and machines.

In a crude way, you can think of *talents* as naturally given and *skills* as something you have to work to acquire. The most effective approach for any one person is to discover where their talents lie, then work to develop skills in that area. *Talents are potential; skills are productive.*

If, for example, you have a talent for getting along with many different types of people, you should concentrate on developing specific skills useful for working with people—i.e., planning and conducting meetings, mediating disputes between different groups, and motivating people to work together successfully as a team.

If your talents are in the artistic area, you should concentrate on learning specific skills such as computer graphics, sketching pictures, molding clay, designing clothes, or working with metals.

Talents are the guidelines for developing your skills, but the skills themselves are more important in expanding your options. If you can play the guitar, operate a shortwave radio, grow orchids, sell products or services to others, or write short stories, you will have more options available to you than will people who cannot do anything special.

As a language teacher once said, "If you learn to speak French fluently, you will eventually see Paris—I guarantee it." The same might be said for Russian and Moscow; Chinese and the Great Wall; Spanish and Barcelona, Acapulco, or Buenos Aires. Specific language skills open doors.

Some skills are worth more than others; other things being equal, you should spend your time acquiring the most valuable ones. How can you decide which ones are valuable? Here are some guidelines.

1. Is the skill part of some occupation? For example, the ability to write clearly is an important skill in many lines of work—newspaper reporter, public relations representative, research scientist, and business executive. This ability is a necessity in any job that involves communicating with others. Consequently, it is a useful skill to develop and, as is true of all skills, development requires practice, practice, practice.

Similarly, the ability to work with tools is an important skill for many jobs. If you can weld, solder, run a power saw, float cement, operate a diesel engine or install plumbing, you have a skill that may give you a head start. Various combinations of a wide range of skills are even more valuable in allowing you to choose future pathways.

You do not have to enter an occupation just because you are skilled in the operations there. If you learn to operate woodworking equipment you do not have to be a carpenter, but if you do have that skill, you will almost certainly have more choices. For example, if you have woodworking skills, you might be asked to help with the construction of a theater set, and that opportunity might open up an entirely new set of theatrical possibilities for you.

2. Will other people pay you to teach them the skill? In deciding which skills are valuable, look around you. What skills are people paying for? If someone will pay you to teach them your skill, one advantage is obvious— you can make some money. There are also other important advantages. As a teacher, you will come to the attention of more people and, as a consequence, other benefits may fall into your lap. If you are teaching photography at the local YMCA and some business executive in your class likes your work, they may think of you the next time a requirement comes up for a photographer on a foreign assignment. A long shot? Sure, but all good things are.

Another important result of teaching is that it builds your self-confidence. To teach others, you must be good enough to be considered an expert. The more such opportunities you have, the more self-assurance you will develop; the more self-assurance you have, the more opportunities that may cross your path. A pleasant cycle.

A third advantage of teaching concerns your own development. Strangely, preparing yourself to teach others almost always means that you are learning more yourself. The more you teach, the more you learn.

3. Will the skill be useful throughout life? Regrettably, many of the skills that we develop as children are merely that—childish skills. Knowing how to work a yo-yo, play pool, throw a Frisbee, or build sand castles are not very useful skills for adults. I am not putting down yo-yos, pool tables, or sand castles; I have spent many hours with

Occassionally everyone should **PLAY** with mud pies, or blow soap BUBBLES or lie on the ground and **LOOK** at the clouds, but do these ACTIVITES for the JOY of the moment.

37

all of them—but long hours of intense practice are best devoted to more "adult" endeavors.

You need not be continually serious; occasionally everyone should play with mud pies, or blow soap bubbles or lie on the ground and look at the clouds, but do these activities for the joy of the moment—a marvelously worthwhile goal—not because they are going to lead to expanded future choices.

If you are going to spend long hours during your youth acquiring some skill, work on something that will be useful to you throughout your life. Athletics offers some useful examples. Although many students spend a fantastic amount of time practicing athletic skills, those skills are not especially valuable later in life. Adults do not often play team sports such as basketball or football, to some extent because these sports are physically rough and our eagerness to participate in them drops quickly around age twenty-five. Further, older people may not have access to the necessary facilities or be able to gather the required number of players for a team sport, and most carry busy schedules and therefore don't have time to practice like they did as a youth.

Having said all of that, there are many recreational basketball, soccer, and hockey teams composed of "mature" players, say, in their forties or older, and they derive valuable exercise and camaraderie from their participation in these teams. However, most of these people were not all-stars in their youth and it was not necessary for them to dedicate their entire youthful lives to the sport to enjoy it as adults.

Individual sports such as golf, tennis, racquetball, squash, and swimming are more popular among adults and participation in them is easier because the required number of players is small. Consequently, students would be wise to learn some of these "carry-over" sports rather than restricting themselves to team sports.

Team sports do offer useful advantages: the thrill of organized competition, the feeling of belonging to a close-knit unit, the disciplines of practice and living up to the expectations of others. Young people need these experiences, especially to help with their sense of belonging with their peers. Team sports have their place.

Still, as people grow older, team sports become less important and many people find to their dismay that they have no carry-over athletic skills. As adults fear failure more than young people do, many adults will not risk new learning experiences. You will likely feel the same way when you grow older, so learn some athletic skills now that will be useful to you later on.

4. Will the new skill help you conquer new environments and gain new experiences? The more different settings that you are familiar with, the more branching gateways will be open ahead of you in the misty future.

If you can think and speak on your feet, you will be called upon more often to lead discussions, give speeches, or organize new group activities.

39

If you can take excellent photographs and arrange them in useful ways, you will have more opportunities for fun and excitement in photographing sports events, organizational celebrations, lively social events, or visiting dignitaries.

If you can speak German or Chinese, or any foreign language, you are more likely to meet people from that country, or even travel there yourself. If a Russian gymnastics team comes to town and you are the only person around that speaks Russian, you are more likely to be invited to the reception; in fact, you may be put in charge—and, with luck, the Russians may invite you for a return visit.

If you can sail and do celestial navigation, you are more likely to be asked to crew on an oceangoing sailboat.

If you can fix small engines, radios, and other gadgets, you are more likely to find work in a research laboratory, or to be invited along on research adventures such as a snow-mobile expedition to polar areas, or a Jeep trip deep into Africa.

To be lucky, you need some skills.

5. Do you like to do it? In selecting a skill to develop, pick something that you like to do; if you do not like it, you are almost certainly not going to be very good at it. Determination can take you a long way; sometimes you can learn to like a useful but disagreeable activity by sticking with it until you are good at it, but that is an exception. If you do not like to do something, work on other skills.

This assumes that you can find something that you like. If nothing appeals to you, if you have never done anything that has really excited you, if you cannot think of any interesting people to imitate, if you are continually passive, unimaginative, and bored with life, then this book cannot help you—probably nothing will.

If you are serious about wanting to experiment with new activities, and thus learn some new skills, but do not know how to begin, here are some suggestions:

- Read magazines—art magazines, car magazines, electronic magazines, financial magazines, scientific magazines, travel magazines—you can find them in bookstores or at the library.
- Study what interesting people do—watch them or, better yet, ask them; they will tell you about their

activity, and will probably be pleased that you asked.

- Spend some money on some new things (clothes don't count here!)—buy a leather kit, or a clock that you can put together yourself, or some new plants.
- Visit a factory, a botanical garden, the backstage of a theater; they are all filled with people being paid to do interesting things.
- Browse hobby shops.
- Volunteer for something—work in a hospital, a prison, a school.
- Become interested in old things. Visit museums and antiques shops. Start a collection of objects that fascinate you.
- Ask other people to explain their hobbies or jobs to you. Most people are delighted to talk about their interests, especially if you can ask intelligent questions. Find out what interests other people, and why.
- Surf the web for knowledge. Increasingly the whole world of information is at our fingertips. Surely you can find something interesting.

41

Your Intellectual Intelligence (IQ)

For years, psychologists have used mental tests to describe what the person on the street calls "brainpower." Generally, it means the person's ability to solve analytic problems. Often it is described by the term, IQ (intelligence quotient), which reflects a specific kind of problem-solving ability, especially working with ideas, mathematics, and scientific concepts. (Another kind of intelligence, usually termed "emotional intelligence" (EQ) is more related to the solving of problems involving relationships between people. More will be said about that below.)

Most students sooner or later have an opportunity to take a mental ability test—sometimes they are called aptitude tests, scholastic ability tests, or intelligence tests—so people usually have some notion of where they stand in relation to the general population. For some purposes this can be important information, but unfortunately it can also be misused. When you have this information about yourself, you should use it, but you should not exaggerate its importance. *No one is ever captive to their test scores.*

1. WHAT IS IQ? (INTELLIGENCE QUOTIENT)

For the most part, mental ability tests measure your ability to handle abstract concepts, that is, your ability to see and analyze relationships between different classes of things such as words, numbers, or ideas. Some of these tests are heavily mathematical in content, others are more verbal, and others are more specific tests that focus on mechanical abilities, musical abilities, or vocabulary comprehension. These basic analytical abilities, which are important for success in most college subjects (especially science and math) are only a few of the many possible mental abilities. Whether you score high or low on a given mental ability test does not automatically mean that you will be a success or failure. Other characteristics, such as imagination, persistence, and empathy for the emotions of others, are at least as important as intelligence.

Analytic mental abilities and their relation to success in life are roughly similar to height and its relation to success in playing basketball. Height is an enormous asset if you are a basketball player, the more of it the better. However, simply being tall is no guarantee that you will be a star. To be an outstanding player, you must not only be tall, you must be in good condition, you must have good coaching, and you must practice, practice, practice. It is the same with mental abilities and success. To be bright, to have a lot of "brainpower," is also a substantial benefit, especially in academic subjects, but that alone will not bring you success unless you (1) are willing to exercise your mental abilities (get in good condition), (2) seek out good teaching (coaching), and (3) are willing, even intensely motivated, to practice, practice, practice.

2. CAN YOU IMPROVE YOUR IQ?

Can you improve your mental abilities? Like your height, within limits, there is not much you can do after your childhood days to increase these capabilities. Whether the development of mental abilities in young children can be accelerated is still an open question. Apparently, if children in their early years, say under age eight, are given a healthy diet and a great deal of early stimulation through books, imaginative television programs, nature trips, visits to museums, factories, offices, and libraries, their mental processes will be better developed that those of children who are denied such early stimulation.

After about age fifteen or sixteen when the rate of physical growth slows, so also does the rate of growth in mental abilities; from that point on, a person's standing on measures of mental ability in comparison with other people remains about the same for many years. Still, all is not lost. Even though your basic mental abilities do not expand much past age sixteen, they can always be put in better shape, just as your physical body can always be better conditioned, no matter what your height. Some people take good care of their bodies; they exercise regularly, they eat healthy foods, they do not smoke or drink to excess. Consequently, their bodies, when called upon to perform, do much better that do the bodies of people who do not take care of them.

Many good basketball players are not particularly tall; they succeed through some other talent such as quickness or dexterity ("good hands") or through fantastic determination and hard work. In the same way, many people with modest mental abilities, as measured by the tests, can be successful. Does that mean that the tests are no good? No, it means that there are other talents that are also important. Just as a tall, lazy basketball player will not be successful, neither will someone who is lazy about developing their special talents.

The same is true of mental abilities. During our teenage years, our abstract intelligence—in terms of power to handle words, numbers, and other abstract topics—reaches the general level where it will remain for the rest of our lives. But, like our bodies, we can even keep it sharp by regular practice and stimulation, or we can let it deteriorate through lack of use, and then be disappointed when we to call on it.

3. HOW TO STAY BRIGHT—KEEP POLISHING.

The best way to keep your mental abilities in condition is to stay active mentally. Keep reading, studying, taking challenging courses, exposing yourself to others who are better educated than you. Keep tackling new challenges. These activities keep your brain from getting rusty.

If you have taken a variety of tests and have some awareness of the results, you can use this information to help you make a sensible occupational choice. Generally, the more complex the occupation, the more mental power you must have to succeed there. People in the most complex occupations—nuclear physicists, medical researchers, federal judges, university professors—are drawn from the highest levels of intelligence, say the top 15 percent. A few people from further down on the ladder succeed in these occupations, but only because they have other compensating assets, such as a willingness to work unbelievably hard, an unusual imagination, good family connections, or, occasionally, pure luck: being at the right place at the right time.

Below this elite corps is a much larger group of people drawn from perhaps the upper 30 percent of the population in terms of mental abilities. Here are the doctors, lawyers, accountants, psychologists, business executives, ministers, social workers, engineers, biologists, chemists, military officers, and other professionals.

Below these come the majority of people, those of average, normal intelligence. The majority of us are average, although this may be hard to accept; no one likes to be considered "average." Yet this is inevitable, because the definition of "average" means the place where most people fall. Being average should not disappoint anyone because even those of us who are most average have a lot of control over our lives. As the famous African American baseball player Satchel Paige said, "Ain't no man that can avoid being born average, but ain't nobody got to be common."

Most of the workers in our society have a normal amount of mental abilities, that is, they fall into the mid-range of the population. Those who work in offices, hospitals, or farms; those who drive trucks, who are police officers, beauticians, salespeople, owners of small businesses—on measures of mental ability these people generally fall within the normal range. There are many exceptions. Some people in these occupations score high on mental ability tests, which means that they have not had the opportunity to move into more complicated jobs, or that they like what they are doing and prefer it over other possibilities, or that they have not stretched themselves. Other people in these jobs may test low on these general measures and yet be successful, which means that they have either had unusual opportunities handed to them which they have successfully exploited or that they have applied themselves with unusual dedication, climbing farther up the ladder than have others at the same level of general mental ability, perhaps because of their adroit use of "common sense."

People with lower scores on measures of intelligence, those below average, usually end up in less complicated jobs such as factory work, janitorial work, simple clerical positions, or a wide range of other unskilled jobs. They make useful contributions to society and they usually enjoy their work, but they do not have to deal with the same complexity as do those in higher-level jobs, and of course they are paid less. Even at this modest level of intelligence, people differ a great deal in their imagination, enthusiasm, and dedication to work, and people with modest formal intelligence frequently contribute a great deal through their work.

4. Consequently . . .

Remember these three things about your brainpower:
- If you have it, use it, or you will lose it.
- Aim realistically for a level at which you can succeed.
- Even if you score low, there are other ways to succeed.

Your Emotional Intelligence

Through the 1900s and essentially most of the twentieth century, many psychologists focused on measured intellectual intelligence, which some referred to as the Primary Mental Abilities. Through dissection of this concept, various specific categories appeared, such as mechanical ability,

If you have it, use it, or you will lose it.

vocabulary, fluency with words, spatial ability. Each of these areas seemed to have their own special niche, but they were all embedded in the general concept of intelligence, and fell under the label of IQ.

Then, in 1995, Daniel Golman, a Harvard-trained psychologist who was also a science writer for the *New York Times*, published a book called *Emotional Intelligence*. His book became a run-away bestseller, and considerably expanded the way that psychologists thought about mental and emotional abilities.

Golman argued that, yes, intelligence as it has been measured is important, especially in traditional educational settings, but it is hardly the only factor at work. He pointed out that many apparently brilliant people have had modest careers at best, and some of them have even significantly messed up their lives. In contrast, he drew attention to many people who were dramatic successes even though, by traditional measures, their mental abilities were more modest.

Specifically, he presented other concepts that seemed to be more related to productivity and satisfaction in life than was IQ. Examples of some of Golman's uncovered characteristics were "empathy for the emotions of others," and the "ability to delay gratification."

"Empathy for the emotions of others" refers to the person's ability to understand how other people are feeling about some situation in their lives, such as a significant achievement (perhaps winning a major contest) or a disappointing failure, (perhaps experiencing a failed romantic relationship). Empathy in an individual is especially concerned with their understanding how their actions are impacting the feelings of others, which, incidentally, is especially important for people in leadership positions.

The "ability to delay gratification" refers to the trait whereby an individual can give up some immediate pleasure for more focused, disciplined activities, such as studying a foreign language instead of going to a party, in exchange for the probability of substantially greater success in the future, and thus even more pleasure and satisfaction.

Golman's way of thinking immediately became quite popular, and droves of other psychologists, counselors, therapists, and human resource experts began to focus on his expanded concepts.

In his second book written a few years later, *Working with Emotional Intelligence* (1998), Golman summarized much of this widespread attention into the following analysis:

Emotional Intelligence (EI) can be separated into five components; each one is important, and each one can be improved by study and practice. The five components are:

1. Self-awareness concerns understanding oneself, that is, how aware the person is of their own capabilities, emotions and behaviors, how these factors affect their own life, and especially what impact these personal characteristics are having on others around them. For example, a well-developed sense of self-awareness leads to being aware that if you continually tease and bully others, you are eventually going to create enemies.

The improvement of self-awareness can come about through at least two channels. First, by stepping back, as if you are looking at yourself from above, and analyzing what impact your personal characteristics are having on yourself and on the way you are treating others, and second, by directly asking others, "What do you think about the way I am behaving toward you?" You do not need to become

One, who, inheriting inferior endowments from nature and unpracticed in the duties of civil administration, ought to be peculiarly conscious of his own deficiencies.

—George Washington
Referring to himself in an excellent example of self-awareness, in his inaugural address of 1789

obsessive about this, only to become more aware of the impact that you are having on the world.

2. Self-regulation concerns the individual's ability to look at their own behavior and then to make sensible decisions about what they are doing. It essentially means thinking before acting, then avoiding doing stupid things like taking dangerous physical risks—driving too fast, climbing steep rock faces without proper equipment, swimming alone in dangerous waters, skiing outside of marked boundaries—and it also means developing the good sense to understand that you may have to discipline yourself to forego immediate pleasures for the possibilities of greater future success.

3. Empathy concerns the individual's ability to understand the emotions of other people, and then the skill to treat the other people in a way that conveys this sense of understanding. Empathy can be central for effective teamwork as teamwork usually requires teammates to understand and value each other. Empathy is also important when working in new, unfamiliar cultural settings. To work well in a new setting, such as being an exchange student in another country or a manager in an overseas assignment, it is important to be able to understand the emotions and concerns of others who have not had the same background and cultural experiences as you have had. In such settings, the first goal should be simply to listen, and then to understand.

4. Social Skill concerns those abilities related to persuasiveness, and the ability to find common ground with individuals, teams, or organizations

El que se estima en mucho, se conoce poco.

(He who thinks too much of himself knows himself only slightly.)

—Spanish proverb

who are experiencing stress or change. It is related to empathy, but it is more extended in that the goal here is to not only understand others, but to help them move forward in a new, positive direction, in a sense to be a leader. These skills can be constantly honed, from early in life to the highest ranges of adult leadership positions. People who are early leaders in their school situations have the benefit of an early start; others may be "late bloomers." They may begin to develop these skills later in life, perhaps after getting an initial grounding in some technical skill, and then moving into a managerial position, and then into higher levels of leadership. As our society continues to learn more about the importance of leadership skills, training programs to improve these skills have become increasingly frequent for even those in the highest levels of leadership. If you can

51

start young on these social skills, you will be well served later.

5. Motivation concerns the individual's drive to achieve, to make good things happen, to work toward a desired goal. Persistence is important here, as is durability in the face of failure. Lack of motivation is a substantial barrier for anyone who wants to create a productive, satisfying future for themselves. If you do not really want to succeed, the odds are pretty good that you will not.

If you are waiting for a good time, you are wasting your good time.

—**Pakistani teenager**

Motivation is so important among these components of self-awareness that it merits an extended discussion here, as follows.

YOUR MOTIVATION

How hard are you willing to work? How persistent are you? How badly do you want to do well? These are questions of motivation. No matter how smart or talented you are, no matter how many opportunities you have, if you are not motivated, you will probably not accomplish much, which means that you will not have many choices in life. No accomplishments, no choices.

What motivates people? What do they want to achieve? How can you increase your own motivation? Psychologists have been studying these questions for many years and have some, but by no means all, of the answers.

Here are some of the basic findings:

1. Different people are motivated by different things. Some people want to make lots of money, others want to make great scientific discoveries, others want to help people, others want to create works of artistic beauty, and still others want to be part of close knit teams that confront physical challenges such as those that police officers, firefighters, and military officers face. Activities that seem incredibly stimulating to one person may be totally boring to another. Consequently, the secret is to find those activities that attract you because you will never be particularly motivated until you find an activity that is important to you.

2. Almost everyone is motivated when they feel that they are doing something worthwhile. No one likes to feel that their work is worthless, that no one else appreciates them. Consequently, find something to do that you think is worth doing, something that adds some value to others, something that makes our society stronger. A strong motivation can be engaging in activities that are valued by others, such as a wide range of volunteer activities.

3. The more that people understand the value of what they are doing, the more motivated they are for doing it well. Similarly, the better they understand what their individual rewards will be, that is, "what's in it for me," the more motivated they will be. One implication of this is that people who are regularly receiving positive feedback on their performance tend to be more motivated.

This is a point worth stressing. People who do not understand the importance of their activities are not very motivated. Many times students are not aware of the benefits of doing well, so they do not try very hard. "What's the use of getting good grades?" they might say, "I'm never going to use this stuff anyway."

Sometimes they are right, but usually they simply do not understand why what they are learning will eventually be important. If you are a student at any level, do not be shortsighted. Look ahead. The better that you understand the challenges of adult life, the more you will understand why practically all learning is important.

4. People tend to be consistent in their level of motivation; for example, those students who do well in high school tend to be those who do well in college, who in turn tend to do well in advanced study such as law, medicine, or graduate school. People who do well in one task tend to do well in others; people who do well in one job tend to do well in others.

There is substantial consistency in human performance and, to the extent that you can, you should try to succeed in whatever you attempt. Success tends to become habitual.

5. We tend to perform at about the same level as those people who are close to us. Groups of people working together usually set up informal "norms" of performance, that is, expectation about what constitutes a "normal" level of performance, and group members reinforce these norms, usually in subtle ways. Workers on an assembly line, for example, usually reach an understanding, often unstated, of how much work they consider to be fair. The group subtly disciplines any worker who gets overeager and tries to exceed the norms. "Rate-busters" as they are sometimes known, are brought into line so that they do not embarrass the rest of the group by showing them up.

The same phenomenon occurs in many other settings. Among some students, doing too well is sometimes looked upon with great distrust. In some groups, a person is supposed to be happy with a "gentlemen's C," with the implication that anyone working for a better grade is no gentleman. A whole vocabulary has grown up to describe this student; the words change with new generations of students but the sentiment is constant—"apple polisher," "curve-raiser," "brownnoser."

The same situation exists in the world of work. People in different settings have different expectations of themselves and their coworkers. In some places, people expect a great deal from each other; they stimulate each other, they encourage each other, they urge each other on to greater heights of achievement. In other settings, people hold each other down by tolerating shoddy work, or by not expecting very much of each other, or by even subtly punishing anyone who attempts to stand out.

The implication for you as an individual is that you ought to seek out a place where you will be encouraged to achieve—assuming, of course, that achievement is important to you. You should seek out those situations where you will be stimulated, not deadened. Usually, this means finding people who are better than you and trying to raise yourself to their level.

The basic point is that the people you work with are going to have a substantial impact on your motivation. If you want to be motivated to achieve, the choice of your co-workers may be the most important choice that you make. Stay away from the rumdums; they will drag you down.

YOUR FRIENDS

Along with your coworkers, your friends are going to be an important factor in your life, especially in what you will accomplish and the resulting choices that you will have open for you.

Parents are always worried about the kinds of friends that their children have, and sometimes the children feel overprotected. What your parents know now, and what you will eventually learn, is that hardly anything influences our lives as much as the people we associate closely with. There are many reasons for this but one of the most important is that we continually use other people for models. We use them as guides for our own actions, and close friends prove to be some of our most powerful models.

1. What kind of friends do you want, and why?

Look around you. The general life that you are going to have will probably be similar to the life that your friends are living, partially because you will consciously or unconsciously model your life after theirs. You will probably dress the way that they do, like the same music that they do, and engage in many of the same activities as your friends do. If they engage in unhealthy activities, there will be pressure on you to do the same. If they are creative and achieving their goals in many different areas, this will encourage you to do likewise.

For prediction of your future lifestyle, you might look at your parents and the parents of your friends. They offer the best guess of what your life might be like in the future. The prediction is far from perfect, but it is the best one that you can make now. Is it appealing to you? If not, what might you do to have your life come out differently?

2. You will probably, subtly, become more like your friends.

No matter what group you choose to associate with over the next several years, you will likely become more like the members of that group in your attitudes, opinions, and actions. They will become more like you, too; the influence works in both directions.

A specific example: a young man who is majoring in, say, art, and who moves into a dormitory dominated by students majoring in another subject, say, science, will tend to change some of his attitudes in the scientific direction. If he lives in the dorm for a long time, he will likely develop more positive feelings toward science than will other art students who only associate with art students. He may even change his major to science as he learns more about what attracts his dorm mates to the subject or, perhaps more likely, will choose some intermediate major such as computer graphics. Over time the minority tends to change to become more like the majority. The changes are not necessarily large and are by no means certain, but the general tendency is there and it will likely happen to you in a similar situation. Over the years, you are going to change to become more like the majority of your friends, and they will change to become more like you.

An important implication is that you had better choose your friends fairly carefully, because this is one way of controlling your own development. By putting yourself in close contact with people whom you would like to be like, you are apt to change in ways that will please you.

3. A caution: Be careful around losers.

If you associate with people with self-inflicted problems, you are likely to find yourself with similar problems. If your friends are a bunch of losers, if they are always in trouble because of misbehaving, if they are overweight and out of shape, if they never have any money because they foolishly spend the money that they have, if they are frequently drunk, or smoke a lot, or use hard drugs, if they constantly have trouble in school, if they waste hours every day watching television, if they try to solve many of their problems by "being tough," then you are likely to slide into those same patterns. Through these kinds of friends, you can pick up a significant number of liabilities and very few assets. The ancient adage, "Birds of a feather flock together," is well supported by psychological research.

Fortunately, the other side of the coin is also true. If your friends are talented, if they get good grades, if they are thoughtful toward others, if they are good athletes and keep their bodies in good shape, if they do not smoke and handle alcohol and other drugs reasonably, if they are happy and cheerful, if they are involved in healthy pursuits such as singing, dancing, athletics, environmental programs, scientific contests, useful hobbies, or good jobs, then you are more likely to become involved in the same activities.

Although these comments are geared toward students, the same factors operate throughout life. Whether you are seventeen, thirty-seven, or sixty-seven, your friends are going to have a sizeable impact on you, especially in developing your attitudes and opinions. If you spend time with people who value exercise and good health, you are going to keep yourself in better physical condition; if you spend time with people who travel, you will likely travel more; if you spend time with cynical people who complain about their lot in life, you will more likely become more pessimistic yourself; if you spend time with people who contribute to our society in worthwhile ways, you are likely to contribute also.

These are only probabilistic statements; each of them should be prefaced with the phrase, "The chances are . . ." but the trends are fairly strong. Good friends can be wonderful assets; poor ones can set you back for years.

4. Be your own best friend, first.

One more thing you should know about friends. Often the people who do best with friends are the people who need them least. If you need your friends as a crutch, in that you constantly lean on other people and cannot stand upright on your own, if you take from friendships more than you give, if you seem "needy" to your friends, you will not be a welcome addition to most circles. Regrettably, in this as in so many other areas, those who need friends the most may have the fewest.

Finally, to gain a friend, be a friend.

YOUR EDUCATION

One reason education is so important to you is that it creates many of the other assets listed earlier. If you have a good education, you automatically accumulate useful skills, broadening experiences, and stimulating friends. Consequently,

59

> **Genius**
> **without education**
> **is like silver**
> **in the mine.**
>
> —Benjamin Franklin

when planning your career, pay a great deal of attention to education, for it is a good way to increase your options. For most people, it can be a lot of fun. Many people will tell you that the years they spent in school were among the best years of their lives.

There are three particular points that you should pay attention to in planning your education.

First, you should study something that you enjoy. If you are having trouble deciding what that is, give yourself a few years to try out several areas. Take some solid basic courses—history, science, languages, mathematics, business, art—in which you will learn a lot about many fields; especially choose courses that will build your assets. A good school counselor can help you decide which courses will be useful, no matter what you eventually decide what to do. Hopefully, this book will give you some ideas too. Generally, the more rigorous the course, such as science or math, the more useful it will be later on in expanding your assets.

Do not worry if you have not yet found an area that excites you; many people take several years to settle in. But do worry about trying new, diverse areas. Keep experimenting with new fields; do not just sit on your hands.

Second, you should go to the best educational institution that you can afford and that you can get into. There are several advantages in going to a good school: (a) you will probably get a better education; (b) you

60

will be surrounded by capable, stimulating people and, as we have already seen, the quality of people that you associate with is going to have a direct impact on the kind of person that you will become; (c) the reputation of the school that you attend is going to affect the pathways that eventually open up to you. A degree from Harvard is going to give you more options than a degree from Southwest State Community College, unfair as that may seem.

Even so, all is not lost. In one research study, eventual advancement in life proved to be more related to class standing than to the quality of the institution. Success in one situation breeds success in subsequent ones.

Third, consequently, wherever you go, you should try to do well. The better your grades, the more options that you will have later, partially because you will have learned more than the average student. Further, and more importantly, if you do not learn to discipline yourself in school, you may not be able to discipline yourself later in life.

Curiously, this last point—doing well in school—may be more important than going to an outstanding school. Students who earn outstanding records in mediocre schools do as well or better in life as do average students from the best schools. I saw this demonstrated vividly when I was on the faculty of the University of Minnesota. When we studied the performance of valedictorians from all Minnesota high schools, we found that the top students from the average high schools in the state did better than did average students from the best high schools.

Similarly, when a major corporation did a study of their higher level executives, they found the same pattern; those who had graduated in the top third of their class from average colleges were doing as well or better than others who

61

had graduated in the middle of their class at the most prestigious universities. One likely explanation of these results is that success becomes habit-forming. Good students in average schools learn to do well, and they learn to expect top performance from themselves. When they move on into other settings, their aspirations for top performance continue.

Your Family

When you are young, your family has more influence on you than any other factor in your life. Even when you are older, family influence is still strong. Most of us vote the same way as our parents, go to the same church as our parents, eat the same kind of foods as our parents, and on and on. In many ways, we are (and are still becoming) what our parents are.

Consider your family as an asset. Not only can your family influence your other assets, but family members can be an important asset in themselves. Family connections can open doors, family skills can be passed down from generation to generation, families can provide experiences for their children, for example, travel, that would be impossible for the children to have otherwise.

Some people get along well with their parents; in other families there are conflicts. Perhaps you may think your family is not much of an asset. You may be right . . . or you may just need more perspective. As Mark Twain said, "When I was a boy of fourteen, I thought my father was one of the stupidest mortals to walk the face of the earth; when I turned twenty-one, I was amazed to see how much the old gentleman had learned in seven years." We all go through some phase of rejecting our parents and perhaps wishing that we had been born into a different family. If that happens to you, try to realize that the other family you want to be born into may be having many of the same troubles that you think you see in your family.

The purpose of this book is to encourage you to look at your situation systematically and to act to improve your assets, therefore your future choices. Where your family is involved, how can you do that? How can you use your family to increase your skills, or your motivation, or your education?

There are several ways.

First, ask them. What are their ideas about the important choices that you are facing? You may be surprised by how helpful your parents and other relatives can be, if you give them the opportunity.

Second, learn whatever skills they can teach you. If they can cook, adjust carburetors, program computers, do macramé weaving, operate ham radios, or understand the stock market, you have a wonderful resource right in your own home. Tap it.

A personal note here: my grandfather was the local railway station agent in the small Iowa town where I grew up. As trains have a certain fascination, I spent many hours at the depot. I often watched him use the telegraph, tapping out Morse code about various train movements, railway car contents, and other related topics. He never offered, and I never asked him to teach me how to send Morse code. I have always regretted that.

Third, utilize whatever material assets are available from your family. Some families,

63

because of their financial holdings, can create significant opportunities for their children. An obvious, and extreme, case is that of parents who can pass on a farm, ranch, or commercial firm to their children; without such a boost, most young families would have a great deal of trouble starting up these holdings on their own. Look into that, or related opportunities, in your family. If your family is in business, study the business thoroughly before you decide whether or not you wish to continue in it. In particular, do not reject it until you understand everything that is involved. You may have more opportunities close to home than you realize.

Fourth, however, be good for something *before* you use your family assets. If you do inherit something worthwhile from your family—whether it be money, a business, land, or a famous name—recognize those resources for exactly what they are, that is, available assets that you can use to expand your choices. But also recognize that family assets can be a burden, especially if you confuse them with *your own assets* as a person. Through the years, as a psychologist, I have worked with many people who have inherited money or fame, and I have seen the many problems that can result. The people who handle such situations best are those who have initially made honest, solid accomplishments of their own, independent of family help. They have a much better sense of who they are and what they can do than do those who have traded on only family assets.

When I talk with young people who are facing the prospects of inheriting a large fortune, or a famous name, or of being over-shadowed by an incredibly talented mother or father, I strongly recommend that they cut themselves loose for a few years to prove to themselves that they can make it on their own. After they have achieved that self-assurance, they can then walk back into the family circle, secure in the knowledge that they could get

What you don't earn, you don't own.

along without the family resources if they had to. Without such confidence, family assets can become psychologically oppressive. If your name if Kennedy, Rockefeller, Vanderbilt, or your community's equivalent, you are going to have trouble establishing your identity as an independent individual, valuable in your own right, so you had better put the goal of independence near the top of your list.

65

Warren Buffet, creator of one of the world's greatest fortunes, when asked what he intended to do about passing his wealth on to his children, said, "You should leave your children enough money so that they can do anything, but not enough so they can do nothing."

Whatever else you do with your family, use them as an introduction to at least two occupations, that is, the ones that your parents are in. To understand what an occupation is all about is difficult for an outsider, and sometimes almost impossible, but at least your parents can help you understand theirs.

To help you encourage your parents (or aunts, uncles, grandparents, neighbors, or teachers) to talk about their occupations, here are some questions that you can ask. Almost *everyone* likes to talk about their work to someone who is really interested, so do not be bashful about asking.

1. *How did you happen to choose this occupation?*

Many people will answer, "Mostly just by chance—it was an accident." Ignore that. While luck, or chance, plays some part in occupational choice, other factors which people themselves may not understand are usually more important. When people are explaining to you how they first started in an occupation, try to analyze what assets they had going for them. What choices did they really have?

A few people may say something like, "I have known all my life, from the time I was quite young what I wanted to be. My interest started early, and it has never changed. I focused my entire education on this occupation, and I am quite satisfied." In a sense, they are the lucky ones. For more people, it requires searching and experimenting.

2. *What do you like best about it?* Try to get them to be specific. Exactly what pleases them?

3. *What do you dislike about it?* Again, strive for details.

4. *What kind of people tend to do well in your occupation?* What are they like? Pay particular attention to the skills and experiences needed.

5. *Do you do the same thing every day or is there a lot of variety?*

Strangely, two people in what appears to be identical jobs may answer this question quite differently. One might say, "Everyday is pretty much the same," while the other might say, "Oh, there is a lot of variety. No two days are ever alike." It is up to you to decide which is more accurate.

6. *How much money does the average worker in this occupation make?*

You should not ask people how much money they make; they may consider that rude. You can, however, ask them about how much their coworkers make, and they will usually answer freely.

7. *What kind of people do you work with? Do you like them? What about them do you like?*

For most of us, one of the main determinants of whether we enjoy our work is the people around us everyday. Pay some attention to that fact when you are trying to decide which direction to go.

8. *Can you think of some particular event that happened recently on your job that made you feel especially good? Can you tell me about it? Why did it make you feel good?* Again, you are looking for details. Ask some probing questions.

9. *Can you tell me about something that made you feel bad? What was the problem?* Again, details, details.

10. *What does the future of your occupation look like? Will there be good opportunities for someone like me?* Their answers may help you in your future planning.

11. *If I wanted to enter your occupation, what preparations should I be making right now?* If you are contemplating going in their direction, their answers could provide you with extremely useful information for planning your next step.

Try these questions out on several people close to you. You will probably find that you are a better interviewer than you think, and you will learn a lot about each of these

67

people and their work. And you will learn that generally people like talking about themselves to someone who is truly interested.

After you gain some confidence from talking to parents, relatives, or close friends, start asking other adults these questions, especially people in occupations that you are interested in. The better informed you are, the better choices you will make.

Your Experiences

Among your most important assets are your experiences; if you plan them with some foresight, you may gain early assets and relevant knowledge with little cost. That is, little cost in money, but you may pay in other ways. As an enlightened, older acquaintance of mine once said, "Experience may not be worth what it costs but I cannot seem to get it any cheaper." Whatever they cost, experiences can never be taken away from you.

Experiences often happen haphazardly in life; you meet people, you travel places, you try new ways, you grow older. Yet you can also plan your experiences, and you should organize them so that you learn the maximum for them. Do not let things "just happen"; let them happen in a way that you know more about life afterward than you did before.

When you are trying to plan your career, for example, you should accumulate as many job experiences as possible, especially while you are young and can easily explore various possibilities. Try out a variety of jobs, work in many different settings, volunteer for work in nonprofit agencies, help out in a range of classrooms. The more you learn now, the better informed your decisions will be later.

In the next chapter, seven basic types of occupations are described. Here is a brief review of them now, along with some specific ways you can gain experience in each type. These experiences can not only help you make better choices later but, equally important, they can teach you skills that will expand your options later.

Influencing. These are occupations where people influence others, persuading them to follow their vision—leadership positions, sales management, advertising executives, or politicians.

Organizing. These are the occupations that dominate most organizations; people in these jobs are responsible for managing daily activities, such as assigning work assignments, establishing and maintaining budgets, providing data, often financial, that allows the organization to determine how successful it is performing.

Helping. These occupations include those where the individual worker is working closely with other people for the benefit of the other people—teaching, healing, and guiding them in their spiritual beliefs.

Creating. These are creative occupations where people work with words, art, music, or any of a variety of artistic design activities, such as fashion design, interior design, and furniture design.

Analyzing. These are scientific and laboratory jobs where people study how the world is put together, usually with an emphasis on mathematics.

Producing. These are "hands-on" occupations, such as the skilled trades or technical jobs, frequently involving work with tools or machines.

Adventuring. These occupations are highly active physically, often competitive, and may involve some sense

69

of physical risk, such as in athletics, military activities, fire protection, or police work.

Your Appearance

Like it or not, the way you look is going to have some impact on your career. Psychological research has firmly established that our reactions to other people are affected by their appearance; we tend to think more positively of attractive people, which means that attractive people have more options available to them than do unattractive ones. In commenting about the restricted opportunities available to the latter, a newspaper columnist once put it cryptically, "Her face was her chaperone."

This may not seem fair—you may think that people should respond to what the other person is really like deep inside. After all, beauty is only skin deep, right? True enough, but for many purposes skin deep is deep enough.

1. ATTRACTIVE PEOPLE HAVE AN EDGE.

Attractive people have a slight edge on the rest of us. The edge is only slight, but it occasionally makes a difference, and in some occupations—fashion modeling, for example—the edge is all that matters.

Well, you say, looks may be important but I cannot do anything about mine so what's the difference? Not completely true. You can take what you have and make the best of it. You can, for example, control your own weight; many people forgo a considerable amount of their natural attractiveness by being overweight. Stay at a healthy weight; you will look and feel better. Pay attention to how you groom and dress yourself. You need not always look like you are going to the palace ball, but you should not look like you just crawled out of the dungeon either.

One specific reason that you should look your best is that it provides a substantial boost to your self-esteem. We all have a large slice of vanity, and few things make us feel more self-confident than the feeling that we are looking our best.

There are many sources of advice about appearance—books, magazines, and newspapers among them. You should take note of them. Do what you can with what you have; the better you present yourself, the more you will have going for you.

2. BEAUTY FADES.

However, a point that may be reassuring. Several years ago, when I was a professor of psychology studying why people enter various careers, among the many different occupational groups that we studied were fashion models from New York and Paris, some of the most beautiful women in the world. One conclusion that I drew from that research is that it is possible to be too beautiful; extremely beautiful people tend to develop exaggerated opinions of their own value, and this may turn their heads from developing other assets. Many of these young women had received national, even international fame, simply for standing still and having their pictures taken, and not incidentally made ridiculous amounts of money. Although they were handsomely rewarded and their egos were momentarily fed by seeing their pictures on the covers of millions of magazines, the experience did not teach them anything else. When their beauty faded, as it always did,

71

many of them had nothing else to fall back on. They had depended on their appearance to open doors, to give them employment, to give them a sense of personal value; when their beauty went, everything else went with it.

Fortunately, some of these women were planful; they developed other skills such as acting, fashion design, merchandizing, managing others, or, occasionally, politics. Many were also blessed with bilingual talents, perhaps speaking both English and French, which provided them with other avenues of success. Their beauty, along with specific skills, gave the savvy ones among them a head start, and the combination was effective. Beautiful women, and men too, who are also talented will find many future pathways open to them.

3. MORE IMPORTANT BY FAR: YOUR PSYCHOLOGICAL APPEARANCE.

Your physical appearance does matter, but your *psychological* appearance is, in the long run, much more important in impacting the way that other people will react to you. No matter how you look, or how you are dressed and groomed, if you are cheerful, smiling, optimistic, and clearly enthusiastic about your life, you are going to be seen as more attractive.

Conversely, if you are often cynical, scowling, passive, complaining, and critical, others will think less of you.

To illustrate this, try this "thought experiment." Quickly, without giving it much thought, think of two or three people in your life whom you consider "attractive." Now step back and look at them in your mind more closely, or, better, look at them carefully the next time that you

One writer wrote something like, "After a beautiful woman has been in the house for three days, no one notices her."

see them in person. Are they truly gorgeous or handsome, or are they mainly, in the flesh, just nice looking? Is perhaps their attractiveness in your eyes due mainly to their psychological appearance, to the fact that they are unfailingly cheerful, friendly, and optimistic? In many cases, that may turn out to be the case. In fact, some people report, as a result of this experiment, "You know, he is really not that attractive physically, but because he is so pleasant and vibrant to be around, I think of him as 'attractive.'"

The moral here is that an "attractive" psychological appearance at a minimum enhances physical appearance and may even, in the extreme case, trump a physically unimpressive appearance.

And unlike your physical appearance, your psychological appearance is completely under your control.

Your Financial Condition

The way that you handle your finances will have a considerable impact on your future options. Realistically, this is not a book on financial planning; you should seek out

73

Money is like a sixth sense, and it helps you to enjoy the other five.

—Somerset Maugham
British author

information on that aspect of your life from more complete sources. Issues such as savings, investments, mortgages, and insurance are important, and a bit complicated. Find some help early, and establish good financial habits while you are young.

However, I will make three observations here.

1. Debt, with the probable exception of home mortgages, is hardly ever wise; avoid it when you can. In particular, *do not use your credit cards to live at a higher standard of living than you can afford.*

2. There is hardly anything more magical than tax-deferred compounded interest; let me explain with an example:

Let us say that a set of twins, Maria and Robert, early develop two different approaches to savings—Maria does,

Robert does not. As a result, when she turns twenty-one and has a full-time job, Maria begins saving $1,000 per year into an Individual Retirement Account (IRA). She does this for ten years and then stops. (In actuality, she probably would not, but assume this for this example.) At that point, Robert, who is thirty-one, starts putting $1,000/year into an IRA, and does so for the rest of his life. The astonishing result: He will never catch up with Maria! Not only that, he will continue to fall farther and farther behind!

The reason is that the accumulating interest on Maria's money in the first ten years will become larger than $1,000 each year, thus exceeding Robert's contribution.

> # Financial security does not come from making money; it comes from saving money.
>
> **—Vice president of a major financial institution**

(This example is based on an assumption of a reasonable rate of return on their investments.)

3. My third observation has a sad tinge to it. On September 11, 2001, the two towers of the World Trade Center were destroyed by a terrorist attack. Almost three thousand people died. Because this was in the center of the New York financial district, many high-level executives, making very high salaries, were killed. From this terrible tragedy came two surprising and disturbing financial observations:

One, although many of these executives were making six, even seven, digit incomes, they and their families were apparently living on the edge of a financial precipice. While they were making tons of money, they were apparently spending even more—on multi-million dollar homes, fancy cars, elegant jewelry, large yachts, private schools for their

> **Money** can't **BUY**
> **happiness,**
> but it **helps you**
> **look** for it
> in **interesting**
> **PLACES.**
>
> —**Attributed to many people**

children, and expensive vacations. When the family's major wage earner was killed, the cash flow stopped. They were left with the expensive lifestyle and often with considerable debt. Thus, at least some of the families received a double blow—loss of a loved one and an extreme financial crisis.

Two, a related outcome. Among some of the families, the major wage earner, usually but not always the father, had been the only one who was aware of the family's finances, including such issues as savings, debt, life insurance, and related issues. Some spouses had been completely unaware of their family finances—had never seen a payroll check, had never paid the bills, and knew nothing about their resources and their obligations. In a few cases, they had apparently never even balanced a checkbook. They lived on credit cards.

Of course, these are extreme examples, and not typical of the usual situation. Still, if this was true of families with high incomes, the odds are high that the same dynamics were plaguing people with more modest incomes.

The financial moral: Start early, avoid debt, and pay attention.

> **I** actually don't care
> much about **money,**
> but it **settles**
> my **nerves.**
>
> —**Joe Louis**
> Former Heavyweight Champion of the World

Your Health

Good health is your most important asset; without health, your other assets become almost irrelevant. Fortunately, in our society good medical advice and information is easily available. Most people have a family doctor or clinic available. In addition, doctors and health scientists write columns for newspapers, magazines, and websites, and many institutions have public health services such as nurses in schools or medical offices in industrial plants. Other experts, such as exercise physiologists, write articles aimed as athletes or others who are interested in maintaining good physical condition. Good information is widely available and can be very useful if you will pay attention to it.

Four potential health problems are so prevalent in America that you need to pay special attention to them in planning your life. Hopefully with prior planning you can avoid these health problems that plague so many people: 1) obesity, 2) lack of exercise, 3) drug dependence (mostly tobacco and alcohol), and 4) stress.

OBESITY

Experts say that almost two-thirds of the people in America are overweight, and almost half of these qualify as obese. A day at the beach is enough to validate such statistics. Being overweight has several disadvantages. One is that overweight people die at a younger age. In planning a successful career, death is a definite handicap. Further, studies say that overweight people do not advance as far in the world as slender ones. The National Association to Advance Fat Acceptance, a San Francisco-based advocacy organization, says that overweight people earn salaries 10 to 20 percent lower than their thinner colleagues and are less likely to receive promotions than slim people, regardless of their job performance.

How do you avoid obesity? Two main ways, simple in concept but difficult in execution: watch your eating habits and exercise regularly.

Many useful books have been written on the subject of diets; one possibility is *Eat, Drink, and Be Healthy: The Harvard Medical School Guide to Healthy Eating* by Walter Willett, M.D. Another recent one is Andrew Well's book, *Eating Well for Optimum Health: The Essential Guide to Food, Diet, and Nutrition.* Find one of these books, or one like them, and educate yourself about diets and eating.

One curious finding: The more people who are around you when you are eating, the more calories you will consume. People eating alone tend to eat less than people in a group, and the larger the group, the more calories people consume, on average. Part of the reason may be that large groups tend to be associated with holidays and celebrations, such as wedding receptions, birthdays, and other celebrations. Simply being alert to this dynamic may help you rein in your appetite.

Fat, drunk, and stupid is no way to go through life, son.

—A famous line from the raucous collegiate movie *Animal House*

Recognize one further crucial point: The eating habits you grow up with are probably going to follow you for the rest of your life so you should begin early to develop the proper ones. Still, no matter how old you are, you can always raise your awareness of the relationship between your eating habits and your health.

Lack of Exercise

Even if you eat well and keep your weight within normal limits, you can still abuse your body by not being active. Unless you engage in energetic activities early in life and maintain them into adulthood, you are likely to lapse into a sedentary life that includes too much television and not enough sweat. Learn to do something active *every day.*

Just
move
more.

Walk briskly or jog, swim, bicycle, or play tennis or racquetball. Do calisthenics also if you can, but my observation is that most people find them repetitive and boring. You need to find activities that you can stay with. Energetic daily walking is an excellent choice.

There have been hundreds of books written about various kinds of exercise, and many of them provide excellent advice. Most of them have, in one way or another, a simple common theme, "Move more." There are specialized exercises that are good for specific purposes, but for most of us, the most relevant advice is "Stay Active." or as one exercise physiologist has said, "Just move more."

If you spend most evenings and weekends sitting in an armchair, watching television, or sitting at a desk, reading, writing, or studying, sooner rather than later, your body will likely fail you. If you always take the elevator even when going up only one flight, if you always take the escalator even where there are stairs right beside it, if you always take the moving sidewalk even when there is a walkway right beside it, if you never engage in any regular physical exercise such as aerobic exercises, enthusiastic dancing, athletic challenges, active gardening, or taking a few brisk walks each week . . . well, you will eventually learn the power of the maxim, "Use it or lose it." You will prematurely age, your muscles will weaken, your breath will shorten, your heart will become weak, and the quality of your life will suffer. Again, this is an area of life where early ingrained habits will likely remain with you life long. If you are a teenage couch potato, without active intention, you will likely be a middle-aged couch potato, and then an unhealthy senior-citizen couch potato. Every day you have a few opportunities to be active instead of sedentary. Again, use it or lose it.

Your main object should be, simply, to move more. Take the stairs instead of the elevator, walk beside the moving sidewalk, not on it. Everyday you have a few opportunities to be active instead of sedentary. Pick the active choice and years from now the beneficial impact will show.

Friends are important here also. Pick yourself some active ones. If your friends care about staying in shape, you will be more likely to. If they are active, you are more likely to be. If they play tennis or racquetball, pickup games of basketball or volleyball, or ride bicycles long distances, you are more likely to do so with them. If you socialize with overweight friends, you may find yourself carrying around their weight also. You will go to too many parties where beer and unhealthy snacks are the norm; thus, you will tend to drink too much and eat too much rich food. Overweight people usually eat and drink a lot, and you will be doing the same. If you want to watch your waistline, watch those of your friends.

And be ruthlessly honest about your destructive habits here. We all kid ourselves that "Just a little won't hurt; it will never show." As an observant writer once said, "The ingenuity of self-deception is inexhaustible."

The **ingenuity** of
self-deception
is inexhaustible.

—Hannah Moore

Drug Dependence

Roughly one person in five still smokes in America, despite overwhelming evidence that smoking leads to serious diseases such as lung cancer, heart attacks, and emphysema. Most smokers start young when they believe that their body is indestructible, and then later on, when many of them want to stop, they are hooked, even though they know that they are ruining their bodies and shortening their lives. Take a lesson from them; it is much easier never to start than to break what many people find to be an unbreakable habit.

If the health issues are not persuasive, perhaps economics will be. With the sizeable increases of taxes on each pack of cigarettes, smoking is an expensive habit. Calculate how much more money you would have at the end of the year if you had not been a smoker. You will likely be astonished by how much you have spent on this undesirable habit.

Vanity may provide another incentive. Smoking ages your skin, creating wrinkles prematurely. Again, educate yourself. Notice the heavy smokers around you. They generally look far older than their compatriots of the same age who have taken better care of themselves. How do you want to look when you get older?

Alcohol is another drug that leads to serious health problems. If you are of legal age, a drink now and then— even an occasional blast—does little harm, but millions of people have escalated from a drink "now and then" into alcoholism. Not only do they abuse their bodies, but they run the risk of legal entanglements through DUIs (Driving Under the Influence). Again, it is largely a matter of the wrong habits learned early. If you are aware of the problem and are determined to be cautious, you will likely not have any trouble. Again, your friends can help; if they are aware of the problems associated with "binge" drinking, they will likely be more restrained. Pay attention to your social life in this regard.

There are various other drugs that get people into trouble: marijuana, crack, heroin, barbiturates, and crystal meth. Most young people have already made up their minds about whether these drugs are dangerous, and when arguments are made to try to change their minds, they resist. If you think that marijuana is a dangerous drug, you are obviously going to be careful about using it. If you think that other "harder" drugs such as heroin and cocaine, are also harmless, then any cautions that I raise here will almost certainly not convince you. Consequently, I will not try, other than to say that there are considerable data available about the effects of harmful drugs on your body. If there is a substantial possibility of long-term physical damage to your body, is the momentary thrill worth it? I know that this sounds "preachy," but an occasional sermon on your health may be appropriate.

Your Health: Evolutionary Reality

A few years ago, I heard an endocrinologist (a medical specialist) talk about the effects of age on the performance of the body. She made a fascinating point. As I remember it, it was as follows:

> In an evolutionary sense, our main purpose in life is to propagate ourselves—to have children—to preserve our species. Consequently, we have to grow old enough to bear or sire children, say age seventeen to eighteen, and then we have to stay

alive another seventeen or eighteen years to protect our children until they are old enough themselves to reproduce. Consequently, in an evolutionary sense, after about age forty, we are becoming essentially useless in regard to the preservation of the species.

Consequently, it is no accident that at about age forty, the deterioration of the body speeds up. People start needing glasses, hearing aids, or hip replacements. Their breath becomes shorter, endurance shortens. Minor injuries such as cuts and bruises heal more slowly. The system starts slowly to fall apart.

What this means is that if you tell teenagers, 'If you smoke, drink to excess, eat junk foods, don't exercise and don't get enough sleep, you will ruin your body,' they know you are lying to them. They are doing all of those things, and their body is just fine, thank you.

The bottom line is that at about age forty, the responsibility for maintaining good health falls directly on the individual's shoulders; no evolutionary safe-guard is going to protect you. Which is why the early establishment of good health habits is so important.

Her comments made a big impression on me, and I think of them often, every time I find it impossible "to delay gratification."

How Do You Wish to Live the Last Forty Years of Your Life? Fit or Fat?

The relationship between your physical condition and the quality of your life is represented in the accompanying

Activity, Health, and Aging

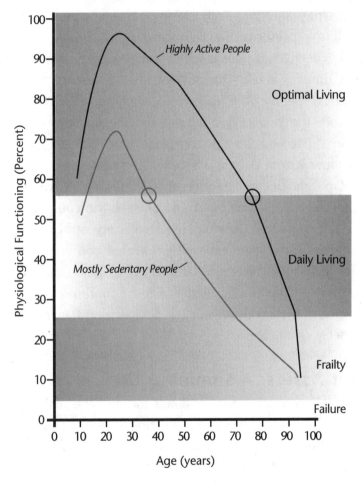

Source: U.S. Surgeon General's Physical Fitness Report, 1996

. . . You'll Probably End Up Somewhere Else

chart which, regarding your future, may be the most important chart that you will ever see.

The horizontal axis is your age; the vertical axis represents physiological functioning, essentially the performance of your body. There are four indicated levels of performance: Optimal Living, Daily Living, Frailty, and Failure. The top line represents the performance of Highly Active People, defined as people who exercise vigorously at least three times a week; the bottom line represents "couch potatoes," people who lead a completely sedentary life.

Note the two circles around the intersections of the "people" line with the "performance" line. What those circles show is that people who exercise regularly remain in the Optimal Living category until they are, on average, about seventy-five years old. In contrast, the couch potatoes sag from the Optimal Living category at about age thirty-five, forty years earlier. How would you like to live those forty years: as young and saggy or older and trim? The choice is up to you. Actually, to be more precise, the choice is in the hands of your self-discipline and your ability to "delay gratification."

Your Assets: A Summing Up

In this chapter, I have outlined some of the major factors that will influence your future choices. No one has all of these assets going for them and, conversely, no one has none of them. As always, most of us fall somewhere in the middle, but with planning and efforts, we can mobilize the assets we have, improve them, and thereby expand the number of choices that we will have in the future.

Again, the same refrain: the more supportive assets that you have—skills, intellectual intelligence, emotional intelligence, motivation, education, stimulating friends, support-ive family, broadening experiences, pleasant appearance, and above all health—the more options you will have in the future, and the more information you will have about your-self and the world, and the better decision you will make.

Sadly, the reverse is also true: fewer assets = fewer future choices.

Recognize your assets, expand them, and you will see potential pathways expanding in your future—and never lose track of the important point made in the first chapter, that no matter how well life goes for you at any given moment, you will never "arrive," you will only be always on the way. Live so that the "way you are on" will be your choice.

87

The law of work does seem utterly unfair— but there it is, and nothing can change it; the higher the pay in enjoyment the worker gets out of it, the higher shall be his pay in money also.

—Mark Twain

CHAPTER THREE

Your Career

·······················

The most important influence on your lifestyle will be your occupation. It will determine not only what you do every day, but it will also greatly affect how you live, who your friends are, what clothes you will wear each day, when you take vacations, how much money you will make, and how long you have to work.

Most important, your work will have an enormous impact on how you think about yourself; we identify more closely with our occupations than with anything else. When people ask, "What are you going to be when you grow up?" virtually everyone answers with an occupation: "I'm going to be a teacher, a politician, an interior decorator, a scientist, or a dentist." No one ever answers, "I am going to be a happy person, a Methodist, and live out West." Although many people will be Westerners, happy people, and Methodists, hardly anyone ever uses such terms to define their future.

Ask an interesting person whom you have just met at a social gathering, "Who are you?" and the response will almost always be something like, "I am a cab driver, a beautician, a lawyer, or a farmer." No one ever says, "I am a lover," or "I am an extrovert," or "I am a five-foot-six, 130-pound parent of three children." Our self-images are dominated by our occupations.

Because your occupation is so important in determining your lifestyle and your self-image, you should give that aspect of your future a great deal of attention, and this is true no matter how old you are. Career choices never stop. Your job will always define you, so you had better closely study the different kinds of jobs.

Some seventy-five years of psychological research has concluded that occupations can be clustered into seven different categories, and every job can be grouped into one of these categories, or some combination of them. In outline form, here are the categories that have emerged from this research.

These categories can be thought as arranged in a circle, as in the accompanying figure, with the categories most alike being located next to each other. The categories most similar to each other are nearest to each other; those most dissimilar are farthest away, opposite of each other across the circle. Each occupation is coded by one, two, or three of the initial letter of each category.

Some jobs fall directly into one category—"auto mechanic," for example, falls into the Producing category, and "office manager" falls in the Organizing category. There are also many combinations. "Art teacher," for example, falls about halfway between Helping and Creating, and "sales manager" falls about halfway between Influencing and Organizing.

The Occupational Circle

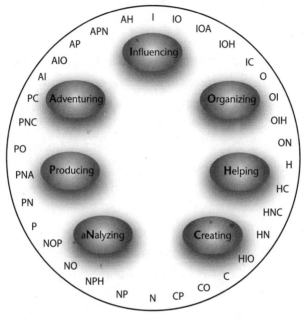

I
Attorney

IO
Financial Planner
Hotel Manager
Marketing Director
Realtor

IOA
CEO/President

IOH
HR Director
School Superintendent

IC
Advertising Account
   Executive
Media Executive
Public Relations
   Director

O
Administrative
   Coordinator

OI
Bank Manager
Insurance Agent
Retail Store Manager

OIH
Hospital Administrator

ON
Accountant (CPA)

H
Guidance Counselor
Religious Leader
Teacher K-12

HC
Social Worker

HNC
Psychologist

HN
Nurse (RN)

HIO
Nursing Administrator

C
Commercial Artist
Fashion Designer
Librarian
Musician
Writer/Editor

CO
Restaurant Manager

CP
Chef

N
Physician

NP
Chemist
Medical Researcher
Engineer

NPH
Math/Science Teacher

NO
Computer Programmer
Statistician

NOP
Systems Analyst

P
Carpenter

PN
Electrician
Veterinarian

PNA
Airline Mechanic

PO
Agribusiness Manager

PNC
Landscape Architect

PC
Architect

AI
Police Officer

AIO
Military Officer

AP
Ski Instructor

APN
Test Pilot

AH
Athletic Coach
Emergency Medical
   Tech
Fitness Instructor

. . . You'll Probably End Up Somewhere Else

In planning your career, you should concentrate on that portion of the circle that attracts you the most, and to do that you need to know more about both the jobs around the circle, and about yourself.

Each of the seven categories, called "Orientations," are described in more detail below by comparing them on three basic ways that occupations differ:

- First, by the work itself on those jobs.
- Second, by the types of coworkers who are attracted to each category.
- Third, by the different rewards provided by each job.

The first difference is *the work itself,* what you actually do all day—whether you build buildings, sell services, manufacture products, or create new things; whether you work mainly with tools, with people, or with ideas; whether you do the work outside, in an office, in a laboratory, or in a hospital.

The second major difference between types of jobs is *the people you work with,* and their most important characteristics will be determined by what they like to do. If you work in a laboratory, you are going to be working around people who enjoy working with lab equipment, usually solving technical problems; if you work in an art museum, you are going to be working around people who like art and beauty; if you work in a school, you are going to be working around people who like teaching students a range of subjects; if you work on a construction site, you are going to be around people who are good with tools and machines, and who have a practical view of the world. If you work in a military unit, you are going to be around people who are disciplined, good team players, and enjoy

> The cure for
> **boredom** is
> *curiosity*.
> There is **no cure**
> for **curiosity**.
>
> **—Dorothy Parker**

physical challenges. Such differences will create quite different work environments.

The third important difference between jobs is *the kind of psychological rewards* that you receive from your work. The psychological rewards do not mean money, but rather the kind of feelings that you will gain from doing a good job. For example, in the Creating jobs, you will have many opportunities to create things, and your satisfactions will come from the thrill of creativity. In the Helping jobs, you will have many opportunities to directly help other people. When you do that well, your reward will be the satisfying glow that comes from watching other people develop in ways that excite them. In the Organizing jobs, you will have many opportunities to help your organization function better. If you do that well, your reward will be the satisfaction of seeing programs run smoothly and your organization being more effective.

The seven categories of occupations are described below in more detail. Recognize that the descriptions are extreme; hardly anyone fits all of these characteristics exactly. When you read these comments, understand that they are referring to general, but strong, trends.

Influencing

These are occupations where people try to lead others, to persuade them to do something—leadership positions, sales management, merchandizing jobs, or politicians.

Influencers are generally confident of their ability to persuade others to their viewpoints, and they enjoy the give and take of verbal jousting.

Typical Influencing Activities
1. Leading an important committee.
2. Giving a speech on your organization's plans.
3. Running for an elected office.
4. Heading up a fund-raising campaign.
5. Participating in a leadership development program.

The Influencing orientation covers the general area of leading and influencing others. Influencers are interested in making things happen; they want to take charge and are willing to accept the responsibility for the results. They typically work in organizations and often want to take charge of the specific activities that particularly interest them. They enjoy public speaking and like to be visible in public. Typical Influencing occupations include company presidents, corporate managers, elected officials, and school superintendents.

Influencing tasks involve persuading other people to your viewpoint. Included are many sales jobs, political jobs, leadership positions, and business executives. Some examples of the daily activities of Influencing people are selling things to other people, running meetings where groups are trying to set standards or arrive at goals, handling situations where new policies or procedures are being debated. Other Influencing activities involve organizing committees, running task forces, planning new organizational policies, worrying about how to motivate others, and planning relationships between people so that their group will be effective. Some other examples of Influencing occupations include business executives, salespeople, political campaign managers, public relations directors, stock and bond brokers, buyers, retailers, fashion merchandisers, and industrial consultants.

Coworkers

People who enjoy working in Influencing occupations describe themselves as "adventuresome, ambitious, argumentative, domineering, energetic, impulsive, optimistic, self-confident, self-motivating, sociable, and talkative."

Such people like competitive activities and like to work in groups where they can have considerable influence over what their group is doing. They see themselves as good leaders and are usually good speakers, both in groups and in one-to-one conversations. They are persuasive, and they enjoy making things happen.

Influencers value money and material possessions. They often drive expensive cars and have expensive hobbies such as sailing large boats or flying their own airplane. Many Influencing people like to belong to country clubs and the best social groups and professional groups; they enjoy trips to resort hotels, often for conferences, and they like to meet and hobnob with famous, rich, and powerful people. In general they tend not to be attracted to science, rigorous analysis, and systematic thinking.

Influencing people usually have a great facility with words, which they put to effective use in selling, leading, and motivating. They are impatient with detail work, or work involving long periods of intense thinking. They like power, status, and material wealth. They have strong drives to attain organizational goals or economic aims. They see themselves as aggressive, popular, self-confident, cheerful, and sociable, generally have a high energy level, and are optimistic, fueled with daily enthusiasm.

96   REWARDS

The unique reward that comes from Influencing positions is the sense of achievement that comes from making things happen, whether it be conducting a successful sales campaign, winning an election, creating an organization that is successful and enduring, or persuading a board of directors to authorize new policies. Influencers generally gain a lot of satisfaction from being where the action is.

Organizing

These are the occupations that dominate most organizations; people in these jobs are responsible for managing the daily activities of most organizations, in setting work assignments, establishing and maintaining budgets, and providing data, often financial, that allows an organization to determine how successful it is being.

Organizers are good with details and usually enjoy solving the day-to-day problems that inevitably appear in organizations.

The Organizing orientation includes activities that bring orderliness, planfulness, and accountability to the working environment, such as managing projects, planning procedures, directly supervising the work of others, and organizing data, especially financial data, that reflect the organization's performance. Organizers generally emphasize efficiency and productivity. They are good with details, and usually enjoy solving the day-to-day problems that inevitably appear in organizations. They understand budgets and cash flow and are often good with investments. Typical Organizing occupations include accountants, financial planners, office managers, and administrative assistants.

Typical Organizing Activities
1. Organizing employees into teams, departments, or divisions.
2. Preparing financial reports.
3. Handling financial resources, perhaps overseeing their investments.

TYPICAL ORGANIZING ACTIVITIES *(CONTINUED)*

4. Planning long-range budgets.

5. Preparing detailed financial contracts.

6. Supervising the work of others.

7. Setting up efficient work systems.

Other organizing occupations include financial analyst, corporate managers, accountants, bank managers, retail store managers, and administrators in many different types of organizations.

COWORKERS

People who enjoy Organizing jobs describe themselves as "organized, conscientious, efficient, inhibited, orderly, conforming, persistent, practical, calm, and comfortable with numbers."

They like their lives to be orderly and organized. They like to know what is expected of them, and they enjoy carrying out assignments. They prefer regular hours for work, and like to work in comfortable, orderly indoor environments. Usually they are averse to free, unsystematic exploratory behavior in new areas.

Organizing people prefer the highly ordered activities, both numerical and verbal, that characterize the necessary, orderly, day-to-day activities that characterize most organizational settings. They fit well into large organizations and seek only those leadership positions directly tied to their work, preferring to work within a well-established, predictable chain of command. They dislike ambiguity and prefer to know precisely what is expected of them. They see themselves as "conventional, well-controlled, and dependable." They have less interest in problems requiring physical skills or intense relationships with others. Like Influencing people, they value material possessions and status, though they usually prefer conforming and subordinate roles.

Rewards

Organizing people like to live a life that is orderly, predictable, and efficient, and they devote their energies toward that end. Consequently, they are gratified when their world fits that definition, especially when the outcome is clearly effective. They take delight in carefully planning ahead, and then creating the desired end result. They enjoy seeing their financial situation improve. Because they are thrifty and manage their money sensibly, making conservative investments, and using their money well, they take great pleasure in watching their investments grow.

99

Helping

These occupations include those where the individual worker is working closely with other people, for the benefit of the other people—teaching, healing, or helping them with their religious beliefs.

Helpers enjoy having close, personal contact with others, and are genuinely concerned with helping their students or clients live full, healthy, satisfying lives.

Typical Helping Activities
1. Teaching someone how to read.
2. Helping a friend through the breakup of a difficult relationship.
3. Organizing a round-table discussion about different religions, with representatives from each.
4. Working with someone who has a severe speech impediment.
5. Advising someone about their career choices.

The competencies involved in Helping occupations are those concerned with working with other people, teaching them, training them, curing them, healing them, organizing them, or enlightening them. Examples of such occupations are high school teacher, speech therapist, physical education teacher, playground director, clinical psychologist, career counselor, and city school superintendent. Helping tasks include explaining issues to others, entertaining people, planning the teaching of students, helping people solve their difficulties, organizing and administering charities, and mediating differences between people.

Coworkers

People who enjoy working in Helping occupations describe themselves as "cooperative, friendly, generous, helpful, idealistic, responsible, sociable, tactful, and understanding." They like to work in groups, especially in small groups that are working on problems common to individuals in their group.

They dislike working with machines or in highly organized situations such as military units. They like to discuss philosophical questions—the purpose of life, what constitutes right or wrong, the causes underlying interpersonal disagreements. They are usually socially competent, and they like situations that allow them to rely on their social values, such as leading group discussions or working with individuals grappling with personal dilemmas.

Helping people are concerned with the welfare of others. They usually express themselves well and work with a wide range of individuals. They like attention from others, and seek situations that allow them to be at or near the center of the group. However, they often prefer small groups rather than large audiences. They prefer to solve problems by discussions with others, or by arranging or rearranging relationships between others. Helping people also describe themselves as "cheerful, popular, achieving, and good leaders."

Rewards

The rewards of working in Helping occupations center around the warm glow that comes from helping other people solve their problems, or watching them improve themselves. People from all walks of life are called on occasionally to help their friends in time of trouble, but people in Helping occupations are called upon daily for that kind of help; indeed, they are usually paid for it—it is their job. Consequently, they often have opportunities to work closely with other people, and they have frequent opportunities to see the results of how their actions have helped others. People in Helping jobs usually have coworkers who are like themselves, and groups of Helping people are usually warm and supportive of each other. They make each other feel wanted, they have respect for each other's abilities, and they have many opportunities for close personal relationships.

The Helping occupations involve coaching and developing others through activities usually related to personal services, such as teaching, counseling, or healing. Helping people are compassionate and deeply concerned about the well being of others. They enjoy having close, personal contact with others, and are genuinely concerned with helping their students, clients, or patients live full, satisfying lives. They readily understand the feelings of others, and can provide emotional support. High-scoring occupations include counselors, teachers, religious leaders, and many health service specialties.

Creating

These are creative occupations where people work with words, art, music, or any of a variety of design activities.

Creators see the world through innovative eyes and are frequently uncomfortable with traditional organizational constraints.

The Creating orientation includes artistic, literary, and musical activities such as writing, painting, dancing, and

TYPICAL CREATING ACTIVITIES
1. Painting someone's portrait.
2. Acting in a play.
3. Taking music lessons.
4. Reading or writing poetry.
5. Designing new clothes, furniture, or advertising copy for new products.

working in the theater, and also various design activities such as interior design and fashion design. People in Creating jobs are interested in, and confident of their ability to create new products, new visions, and new concepts within these creative areas. They see the world through innovative eyes, and are frequently uncomfortable with traditional organizational constraints. They see themselves as free spirits, and are often fluent and expressive.

Typical Creating occupations include artists, dancers, musicians, designers, and writers.

More activities involved in Creating occupations usually involve the creation of artistic products, working with words, music, or other art forms. Examples of specific activities are painting or sketching pictures, composing or playing music, writing or performing plays, and playing in an orchestra or band. Other examples of creating activities are decorating rooms, designing homes, or doing portrait photography.

103

Creating jobs are found in settings such as art museums, art galleries, music departments, interior decorating firms, music stores, theater groups, libraries, photographic studios, radio and television studios, and any place where creative skills are taught—music departments, art departments, theater departments, and often departments of journalism and schools of architecture.

COWORKERS

People who enjoy working in Creating jobs describe themselves as "complicated, disorderly, innovative, emotional, idealistic, imaginative, impractical, impulsive, nonconforming, and original." They like to work in free environments that allow them to express themselves in a wide variety of media—writing, music, drawing, acting, photography, fabrics, and room decoration—in general, any art form or material.

They value beauty and esthetic qualities, and often do not care much for formal, social engagements. They like small intimate groups, and generally do not like large structured "country-club" type affairs. They like to create new and different products and concepts, and are willing to take risks to try something new even if the chances of failure are high.

Many artistic people feel driven to produce their own distinctive product; they like to express their personality in their output, and they feel uncomfortable in settings where they have to inhibit themselves. People in Creating jobs often dress in freer styles than other people; if everyone else is wearing suits, they prefer jeans. If everyone else is wearing jeans, they prefer capes or caftans—something

104

distinctive, something that expresses their personality. They have distaste for appearing conventional or undistinguished. They like to use their creativity to help them stand out from the crowd.

Creative people have little interest in problems that are highly structured or that require a lot of physical strength, preferring those problems that can be dealt with by means of self-expression and artistic media. They resemble Analyzing people in preferring to work alone but they are willing, when the situation requires, to be part of disciplined musical or theatrical groups. Compared with Analyzing people, they have a greater need for individualistic expression, are usually less assertive about their own capabilities and are more sensitive and emotional. They score higher on measures of creativity than any of the other types. Other adjectives that they use to describe themselves are "independent, original, unconventional, expressive, and intense."

REWARDS

The unique rewards of Creating jobs come from the opportunities for creating new things, and from being around other Creating people. In many Creating jobs the person is expected every day to create something new, to try something different, to stretch for new ways. This continual stimulation for the new and different, for quality in creativity, is a primary reward of artistic jobs. Creating coworkers create an atmosphere in which this continual striving for freshness, innovation and distinctiveness is tolerated, and even encouraged.

Analyzing

These are scientific and laboratory jobs where people study how the world is put together, usually with a heavy emphasis on mathematics.

Analyzers have a strong need to be autonomous, to understand the world scientifically, and they like to work through problems for themselves. Analyzers are comfortable with data and numbers and they have a strong need to understand the world in a scientific sense. They usually prefer to work alone or in small groups in laboratory or academic settings. Typical occupations include scientists, medical researchers, and statisticians.

TYPICAL ANALYZING ACTIVITIES
1. Reading scientific reports.
2. Working on new, creative computer applications.
3. Studying blood samples through a microscope.
4. Solving mathematical or statistical problems.
5. Looking through scientific data for basic trends.

The tasks involved in Analyzing jobs are usually scientific in nature and usually involve trying to solve puzzles, whether the puzzle is a large, mysterious problem such as how the universe came into being, or a more normal daily problem such as analyzing the composition of a blood sample taken from a patient in a medical clinic.

Analyzing jobs almost always involve numbers in some way, such as mathematical formulas or a wide array of statistical data. The work usually involves charts and graphs, numbers and formulas, and data about a wide variety of physical phenomenon such as the load-bearing characteristics . . . steel or concrete, or the voting records for each county across an entire state, or the protein composition of various foods. Frequently these tasks require long periods of intellectual effort, and Analyzing people have been known to spend all night or entire weekends working on scientific problems. Indeed, some scientists have literally devoted their entire career to studying scientific phenomena that particularly fascinate them. They become almost obsessed with the need to understand and explain their particular niche of excellence.

Analyzing workers are usually found in research laboratories or clinical settings, but they also work in a wide range of other places—highway departments, where they study issues such as traffic control and composition of highway materials; in advertising agencies, where they study market surveys and consumer behavior; in food-producing companies, where they work on the nutritional aspects of food; in military units, where they develop new weapons or new military strategies for national security; in financial organizations, where they analyze important economic trends such as investment strategies, cash flow, and inventory analysis—in general, any place where problems are being attacked in a systematic, scientific manner.

Analyzing tasks frequently involve the use of computers, microscopes, telescopes, high-speed centrifuges, or any of an impressive array of other laboratory and scientific equipment. Analyzing jobs differ from Producing jobs in that the Producing job is usually more concerned with machines that produce or move around products, while the Analyzing jobs are usually more concerned with machines that produce or manage data and other information.

COWORKERS

People in analyzing jobs are task-oriented, which means that they get all wrapped up in the problem they are working on. For the most part, they are not particularly interested in working around other people. They prefer to work independently, and they usually do not like to be supervised or to supervise others. They sometimes perceive themselves as lacking in leadership or persuasive abilities, but they are confident of their scholarly and intellectual abilities.

They enjoy solving abstract problems and have a great need to understand the physical world; this includes a reverence for "hard data" and a reluctance to accept unquestioningly "traditional wisdom." They enjoy ambiguous challenges, and do not like highly structured situations with lots of rules. They frequently have unconventional values and attitudes and tend to be original and creative, especially in scientific areas. They are often somewhat asocial and do not enjoy large social gatherings.

In many of these respects, they resemble people who are in Creating jobs.

Analyzers describe themselves as "analytical, questioning, independent, reserved and curious."

The unique reward of many Analyzing jobs is the worker's freedom and opportunity to satisfy their innate curiosity. Scientists are continually curious about nature, about people in a scientific sense, about business and especially operational processes, even about art and music, and they are continually studying all of these areas using a scientific approach—analyzing situations, checking out data, trying to understand what is going on in whatever field in which they are working.

In addition, Analyzing jobs usually allow the worker considerable freedom to try out their ideas and theories. These workers are allowed, within reasonable limits, to indulge their own work-styles, though of course within their organizations, there is always steady pressure for achievement.

Producing

These are "hands-on" occupations, such as the skilled trades or technical jobs, frequently involving work with tools or machines.

Producers are usually good with tools, and they enjoy taking on new construction projects or repairing mechanical breakdowns.

The Producing orientation covers practical, hands-on, "productive" activities such as construction, farming, and mechanical activities. Producing tasks usually involve working with tools or machines and sometimes working outdoors, especially on construction sites. The tools might be large, powerful machines such as bulldozers, cranes, tractors, or big trucks, or the tools might be precision machinery

109

Typical Producing Activities
1. Running a large bulldozer.
2. Building a chest out of wood.
3. Cultivating crops with power equipment.
4. Taking apart and cleaning a small engine.
5. Caring for farm animals.

such as X-ray machines or watchmaker's tools. People in Producing jobs might work with wrenches, hammers, surveying equipment, electrical equipment, or construction machinery. Specific activities might involve working on cars, boats, airplanes, pumps, or automatic high-speed packaging machinery. These jobs frequently involve either building something new such as houses, machinery, roads, and bridges, or maintaining such structures after they are completed. Consequently, Producing people usually like to work with their hands, generally enjoy being outdoors, and like to be able to see the visible results of their labors. Producers are usually good with tools, and they enjoy taking on new construction projects or repairing mechanical breakdowns.

Coworkers

People who are attracted to Producing jobs are usually rugged, robust, practical, and physically strong. They usually have good physical coordination, but they sometimes have trouble expressing themselves in written communication or in talking in front of groups of people. They like to work outdoors, and they like to work with machines, especially large, powerful machines. They prefer to deal with things, rather than with ideas or people. They generally have conventional political and economic opinions, and they are often cool to radical new ideas. They enjoy creating things with their hands. They have good motor coordination, but they are frequently uncomfortable in formal settings, and they may lack verbal and interpersonal skills. They usually see themselves as mechanically inclined and are stable, natural, and persistent. They prefer concrete to abstract problems. They rarely perform creatively in the arts or sciences, but they do enjoy building things. Producing people often see the world in straightforward, tangible, and traditional terms. Possessions are often important to them, and they often put their recreational money into cars, boats, campers, snowmobiles, motorcycles, and other mechanical "toys."

Producing people describe themselves in interviews as "conforming, frank, genuine, normal, persistent, practical, stable, materialistic, shy, and socially uninvolved."

Rewards

A unique reward in most Producing jobs is that life appears to be relatively simple and straightforward, and workers can quickly see the results of their labors. The mechanic who is working on a car can see at the end of the job that the car now functions. The carpenter building a house has the quiet satisfaction of seeing the house take shape. The forester harvesting logs can watch the pile of logs grow larger, and at the end of the day can see the results of his labor. The person who is working on a drill press or a lathe can see the material being formed. The machine adjuster working on a high-speed packing line can quickly see the speed at which materials are being processed. In general, on Producing jobs, life is not complicated by intricate problems between people or organizations, nor by troublesome choices between conflicting philosophies.

Typical high-scoring occupations include mechanics, carpenters, veterinarians, and landscape architects.

Adventuring

These occupations are highly active physically, often competitive, and may involve some physical risk, such as in athletics, military activities, fire protection, or police work.

Adventurers are confident of their physical skills, and like to be part of athletic, police, or military teams. They often seek out excitement through the use of their physical skills.

Typical Adventuring Activities
1. Competing in athletic contests.
2. Doing physical exercises to keep one's body in shape.
3. Working closely with teams, trying to improve.
4. Protecting people in physical danger.
5. Working with weapons, especially small arms such as pistols and rifles.

The tasks involved in Adventuring jobs are usually physical, and often competitive. A great deal of training goes into improving the physical performance of people in Adventuring jobs, or of the people whom they are responsible for, such as in coaching athletes. Repetitive practice for both individuals and teams is constant.

The activities in Adventuring occupations are usually quite varied during the day, and are often exciting, even creating an adrenaline rush. The activities are sometimes dangerous, thus there is great attention paid to how to handle crises, with lots of attention given to prior planning in how to deal with emergencies.

Adventuring jobs can be quite "equipment-rich." Adventurers often work with outdoor camping equipment, radios, personal weapons, fire-fighting or police equipment, or specialized equipment used in mountain climbing and rescue operations such as ropes, crampons, and climbing axes. Other equipment that is other found in the presence of Adventurers is athletic equipment of varying types.

COWORKERS

People who are attracted to Adventuring jobs often describe themselves as competitive, disciplined, attracted to activities with daily stimulation, and as caring a great deal about the organizations or institutions that they are part of. They enjoy physical activities, and they like to confront competitive situations. They are confident of their physical skills, and often seek out excitement.

Adventurers enjoy winning, but they are also resilient in defeat. They are loyal, patriotic, and it is important to them to feel that they are providing help to a relevant part of society. They are willing to endure a great deal of repetitive practice, and can endure long periods of physical hardships. When necessary, they can go long periods of time with little sleep, can survive on unappealing rations, and can quickly focus their attention on some physical task that must be performed to solve an immediate crisis. Generally, they can survive these challenges through a strong sense of teamwork with their colleagues. They trust each other, support each other, and protect each other. They occasionally find themselves in life-or-death situations, which builds a strong sense of belonging. Often close camaraderie is more important to them than are the larger goals of their organization.

Many people in Adventuring jobs share some common characteristics with people in Producing jobs; they are emotionally stable, resilient under physical discomfort, and see themselves often as relatively uncomplicated, with a strong sense of good and·bad, right and wrong, and honest and dishonest. They often set physical goals for themselves, and then focus intensely on reaching those goals.

114

REWARDS

A unique reward for many Adventuring jobs comes from the camaraderie of close teamwork, and especially the joy of winning. An attendant feeling is the sense of reaching important goals, of achieving something worthwhile, perhaps of even leaving an historic record behind, such as mountains climbed or athletic contests won.

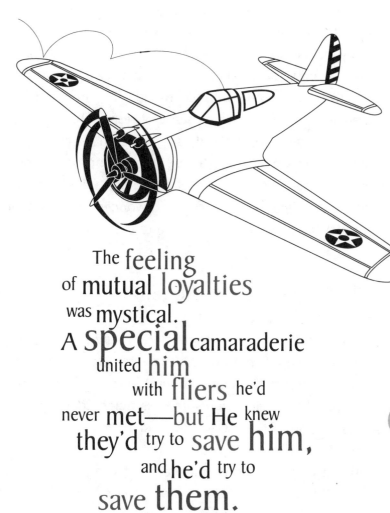

The feeling
of mutual loyalties
was mystical.
A special camaraderie
united him
with fliers he'd
never met—but He knew
they'd try to save him,
and he'd try to
save them.

— Col. Jimmie H. Butler, USAF (ret.)
A Certain Brotherhood

For many Adventurers, especially in police work or military activities, there is also a satisfying thrill of helping people in danger, of making people feel safe. One of the most important feeling in life is the feeling of being relevant. Many people in jobs where they help others in danger, often in crisis situations, or in situations where they are directly protecting our most cherished values from possible enemies, often feel a strong sense of responsibility for our protection and safety. Hardly anything can be more relevant than this basic opportunity to serve and protect others. As a Marine Corps General once said during wartime, "No marine gets up in the morning wondering whether or not they are making a contribution to their county."

The Occupational Circle: A Summing Up

Now that you have some notion as to the various types of occupation and their characteristics, let's review the structure of the world of work, represented by the Occupational Circle, using some examples. Look over the circle on page 91. Note the illustrative occupations listed for each type, or some combination of types. Remember, within each occupation these are only averages; people in each of these occupations are not all alike. This classification system is not perfect, but the trends are clear.

Use the Occupational Circle illustration as a guide to help you learn more about occupations. Focus on that part of the circle that appeals most to you, then set out to learn more about the occupations in that part of the circle.

How do you learn which part of the circle appeals to you most? That takes a little effort. *First*, look at the typical tasks list for each type and decide which cluster appeals most to you. Maybe more than one cluster attracts you; then you should look at occupations that fall between the clusters.

Use the same approach on the other occupational characteristics, such as coworkers, and major rewards. With some study, research, and experience on your part, your personal preference patterns may begin to emerge.

Second, an expanded and more systematic way of looking at your personal choices is to consult with a skilled counselor. Ask to fill in a career inventory, and then discuss your results. These are professionally developed questionnaires that will help you understand yourself in relation to the world of work. One of the more widely used inventories is the Campbell Interest and Skills Inventory (CISS). Your scores on this inventory will help you understand how you compare, in your interests and skills, with employed people in a wide range of occupations. When the match between you and the typical person in an occupation is high, this provides an excellent guidepost for you in seeking more specific information about a targeted group of occupations. The CISS is available on the internet at www.profiler.com.

Filling in an inventory such as this one and then discussing the results with a professionally trained counselor will provide you with a more substantial base for career planning than you might achieve on your own. Do not be reluctant to seek advice from people who know more than you, and who have had more experience than you have had.

Your counselor can also seek more information and an expanded manual for the CISS from the publisher, Pearson Assessments, at www.pearsonassessments.com.

Sophie Tucker, when asked on her **eightieth** birthday about the secret of **achieving** a long LIFE, answered "keep**breathing**."

CHAPTER FOUR

Live, Love, and Laugh

· · · · · · · · · · · · · · · ·

A few main themes have continually run through this book: here is a summary.

First, *you should have some goals*—"if you don't know where you are going, any wind will take you there."

Second, *selecting your goals is a matter of choosing the direction you want to go* in life, not in choosing some specific place where you want to end up. Life is a journey and you are always on the way. You will undoubtedly hit some potholes, some rough stretches of road. When that happens, you should face them with a positive stance. Perhaps you will need to change your direction somewhat. To do that often requires persistence and self-confidence. Here is a motivating thought that came from someone who faced enormous challenges that most of us can hardly imagine, and succeeded:

Be of good cheer.
Do not think of
today's failures,
but of the success that
may come tomorrow.
You may have set yourself a
difficult task but you
will succeed if you
persevere, and you will
find a joy in
overcoming obstacles.

—**Helen Keller**
Though blind, deaf, and mute from an early age,
she learned to read, write, and communicate with
special sign language.

122

Third, the possible directions that you can choose to take will depend almost entirely on your assets. Consequently, *to expand your choices you should be continually cultivating your assets.* You will have to take the initiative.

Fourth, with a possible few exceptions, *your achievements will be won gradually*, not overnight, and you should proceed accordingly. The Persians had a proverb: "Do little

I've always felt
it was not up
to anyone else
to make me
give my
best.

—Hakeem Olajuwon
The first player in NBA history to
accumulate both 2,000 blocked shots
and 2,000 steals in a career.

things now, so shall big things come to thee by and by, asking to be done."

Fifth, more than any other factor, *your job—or more generally, your career—is going to determine how you live.* Thus, give it a great deal of attention and thought. Those in this world who do not work, either by choice or circumstance, often do not amount to much. Often, they do not even like themselves.

Sixth, *basic to everything is health.* Your body is your instrument of life; take care of it. With health, you have a chance for a satisfying, stimulating future. Without it, your future opportunities will be bleak. Developing good health habits early will have important and wonderful implications later in life.

Finally, have fun. *Don't take yourself too seriously.* One of your first goals should be to develop a healthy perspective. Laugh a lot, love, live.

Be glad of LIFE because it gives you the chance to LOVE and to work and to play and to look at the stars.

—Henry Van Dyke

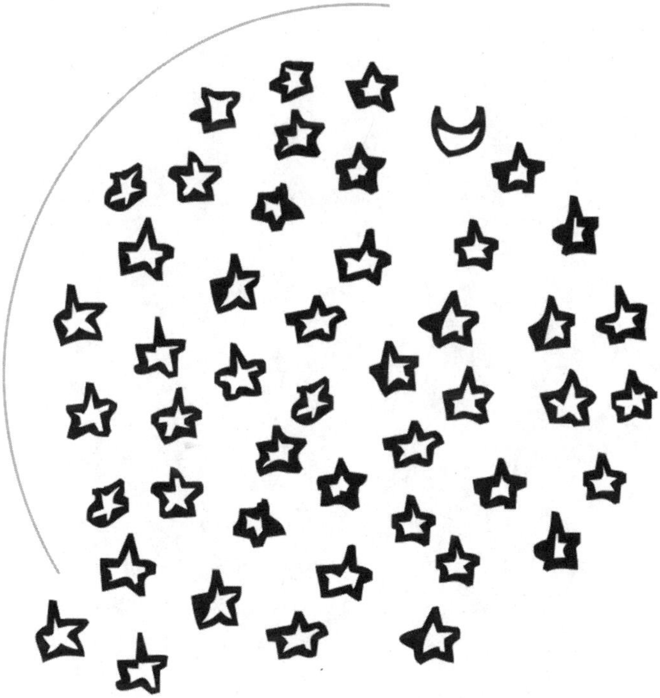

David P. Campbell is an internationally recognized expert in the field of career exploration. He is perhaps best known as the co-author of the Strong-Campbell Interest Inventory, an assessment tool used by many schools to guide students toward career choices based on their personal interests. He is also creator of the Campbell Development Surveys, which include individual surveys designed to analyze interests, skills, leadership potential, teamwork, and working satisfaction.

Dr. Campbell received his bachelor's and master's degrees from Iowa State University and holds a Ph.D. in psychology from the University of Minnesota. He is the Smith Richardson Senior Fellow for the Center for Creative Leadership in Colorado Springs, Colorado. In 2006 he was nominated for the Clifton Strengths Prize for outstanding achievement in strengths-based psychology.

Campbell's other books include *Take the Road to Creativity and Get Off Your Dead End* and *If I'm in Charge Here, Why Is Everybody Laughing?* He is an avid photographer, skier, and squash player.

Other Titles of Interest

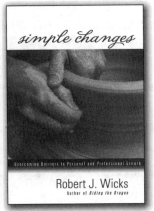

Simple Changes
Overcoming Barriers to Personal and Professional Growth
In this step-by-step guide, Dr. Wicks offers sixteen "seeds of change"—simple yet powerful approaches to encourage readers toward modest, gradual changes in personal attitudes and perspectives.

PAPERBACK ISBN: 1-933495-01-4 / EAN: 9781933495019
160 pages / $12.95
HARDCOVER ISBN: 0-88347-462-X / EAN: 9780883474624
144 pages / $15.95
Sorin Books

Are You Really Listening?
Keys to Successful Communication
Paul J. Donoghue, Ph.D., and Mary E. Siegel, Ph.D.

A thoughtful, witty, and helpful look at the reasons people don't hear one another. With easy-to-learn techniques for becoming a better listener, *Are You Really Listening?* is a guide to listening and being listened to.

ISBN: 1-893732-88-6 / EAN: 9781893732889
224 pages / $14.95
Sorin Books

ave maria press®

Available from your bookstore or from
ave maria press / Notre Dame, IN 46556
www.avemariapress.com / Ph: 800-282-1865
A Ministry of the Indiana Province of Holy Cross

Keycode: FØTØ1Ø7ØØØØ